The Success Guide For Entrepreneurs And Business Owners

BREAKTHROUGH
BREAKTHROUGH
BREAKTHROUGH

HOW TO GROW YOUR BUSINESS
FURTHER, FASTER, EASIER

This book is being given to

_____

Because I care about you and your creating Breakthrough Success in business and in life,

_____

Praise for Linda Feinholz And BREAKTHROUGH

"Breakthrough *is a must read book for success seekers. Linda Feinholz distills the tools, tips and techniques that make businesses grow further, faster, easier and shows you step by step how to implement them for your success in Business and Life!*" Brian Tracy **– Speaker and Author of Maximum Achievement**

"*I just got off of a 1 on 1 coaching session with Linda and she gave me a really easy-to-implement idea that's going to add at least $120,000 to my bottom line this year. I am so glad that I joined her mastermind and her **Inner Circle**, and I cannot wait for the next idea that she gives me.*" **Maritza Parra, Click And Grow Rich.com**

"*As a successful business owner there have been many times in my entrepreneurial life when I was hungry for a breakthrough and just needing to know if my dreams and all my hard work were going to pay off. Then something clicked and an enlightened "Aha!" moment made everything clear, focused, and on track for success. Devour Linda's book, it has proven street smart strategies that will help you avoid the pitfalls while creating the breakthroughs you need to achieve unlimited opportunity and success...this stuff works... I know this as fact!*" Famous Dave Anderson **– Founder of the World's Best BBQ Joint and America's Best Tasting Ribs!**

"*I exited my meeting with Linda and took immediate action that resulted in accolades from my boss, acknowledgement from my team, and a more relaxed successful and excited work environment for all! She's worth her weight in gold!*" Sandy Price **– Leader of a Muliti-million Dollar Sales Team**

"*For the first time in 30 years I went on vacation and didn't think about what was going on in the office ~ I knew everything was under control, being handled, and made more money! THAT'S High Pay-Off!*" **Michael F. Los Angeles**

"*Working with Linda is one of the best ROI's in business! From less than 4 hours a month working with you, learning these techniques* and using these systems, my thinking's been reshaped, my skills have grown by leaps and bounds, and I take action quickly and confidently in new complex situations. We put plans in place and my entire team stepped up in their responsibility and capability. Thanks, Linda!" **Annette Friskopp - Serial CEO and Tech Company Board Member.**

Other Books and Programs by Linda Feinholz

"I Created My Consulting and Coaching Programs So You Can Experience FAST RESULTS for Your Business and Life!

Why Do You Get Fast Results? It's simple… YOU GET ME – My Strategic Experience and Mind Thinking, Working & Creating for YOU & Your Business. Stop Working SO Hard, Wasting Your Time & Money and Spinning Your Wheels Hoping to Figure Out The Direction to Take For Your Business!

www.BreakthroughByDesign.com

You Get Me Figuring Out the 5 D's For You…

1 – **Your Vision & Goals** – We'll **Define** your dream for your life and align the actions you'll take to make it come true, your critical starting point!

2 – **Your Profit Model** – After figuring out your Vision & Goals we'll identify and **Design** how to leverage your "know how" with Ideal Customers.

3 – **Your Systems** – We'll sort out key systems you need to **Deploy** so everything is done with excellence no matter who does it.

4 – **Your Team** – You're probably losing thousands of dollars right now HIDDEN MONEY in your business because you're trying to do things others should be doing for you. We'll **Delegate** those activities *fast*.

5 – **Your Mindset, Skill Set & Tool Set** – Every highly successful person continues to learn and become more confident and capable. We identify the next skills, tools and mindset you need to **Develop** to run your business better and easier, and the best sources to learn from.

That's what I'll create with you!

www.BreakthroughByDesign.com

About Linda Feinholz

Linda Feinholz has dedicated the past 20 years to showing entrepreneurs and executives, business owners and teams how to transform their lives to 'Grow Your Business Further, Faster, Easier' adding 6- and 7-figure new revenue streams to their businesses. Her mission is to guide people to create Breakthrough results - leveraging their experience and expertise.

Linda began her career right out of college. Actually she discovered later that she had started her own Breakthrough career in her teen years, working both in entrepreneurial businesses as well as for large multi-national corporations. In each organization, she saw opportunities to increase the revenue and profits of the business, simplify the operations, and increase the performance of the teams. She continuously distils what worked in one environment and teaches its best aspects it to students, managers, leaders in the next ones.

She owns her own business, speaks internationally in person, on radio and via the internet, has authored over 170 articles, and recorded more than 50 videos and 150 podcasts.

Linda is a **Featured Author** to *The Small Business Book of Lists* series, and in *A Cup of Joe for The Entrepreneur – Women's Edition*. She served as **Associate Editor** for the book *How to Value Your Business and Increase Its Potential* (McGraw Hill). She has published her own books and hosted her own acclaimed radio shows on VoiceAmericaBusiness, ITunes, Stitcher and more.

For a FREE taste of Linda's Breakthrough trainings, visit **www.BreaktheoughByDesign.com/gold**

Book Linda For Your Next Event

Linda Feinholz
"Your Business Growth Mentor"

EVENT QUOTES

"Linda packs the room – standing room only – and keeps the audience engaged. Her energy, ideas, and techniques gets them on their feet."

"Everyone loves her stories, new insights and practical tools to use afterward.

"A *great* addition to any event."

The Ideal Speaker For Your NEXT Event!

How To Use This Book

Had enough with being stalled? Sick and tired of avoiding things that feel overwhelming? Me too! There are plenty of books on increasing your productivity by using kitchen timers and building teams by having people fall out of trees into each others' arms. Large actions and small ones that are all missing the point: We wake each morning to new possibilities, and don't know how to grab them, leverage them, soar with them.

If you want to take your inborn gifts and your learned experiences and expertise and use them to make lucrative results and make a difference in your life and the lives of other people you need to make Breakthroughs – in thought and in action, individually and with your teams.

This book gives you simple, practical, proven techniques and systems that will solve your overwhelm, help you set your Vision & Goals in life and in business, and then Align Your Efforts to achieve them in ways that have you leaping out of bed looking forward to what you'll create in the world. More than just a tips book, each of the ideas is a Building Block you can put to immediate use. In addition to information that will bend your thinking and habits, you'll find Action Plan pages with each topic that will help you track your "Ah Ha!"s and commit to implementing them. And create your "New Normal."

Record your "Ah Ha!"s and Breakthroughs, then tailor each tool to *your* needs as you read them. Discuss them with colleagues, team members, with coaches & partners.

Remember, it's not what you know – it's how you think and what you DO that is the source of Breakthroughs!

~ Linda Feinholz

The Success Guide For Entrepreneurs And Business Owners

BREAKTHROUGH

HOW TO GROW YOUR BUSINESS
FURTHER, FASTER, EASIER

The Tools & Techniques Every Business Owner Needs
To Know To Get Through The Breakdowns and
Obstacles Holding You Back

LINDA FEINHOLZ

BREAKTHROUGH: The Success Guide For Entrepreneurs and Business Owners
Copyright © 2012, 2014 by Linda Feinholz

Library of Congress Control Number 2011941416

ISBN: 0-978-0-98467-725-2 (hardcover)
ISBN: 0-978-0-98467-729-0 (paperback)
ISBN: 0-978-0-98467-726-9 (EPub)
ISBN: 0-978-0-98467-727-6 (EReader)
ISBN: 0-978-0-98467-728-3 (Audio)

Published by:

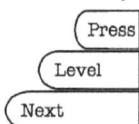

Press
Level
Next

10 9 8 7 6 5 4 3 2 1

Table of Contents

Acknowledgements x

Dedication xi

Introduction xiii

Chapter 1 – Mindset...................................... 1

Chapter 2 – Vision 23

Chapter 3 – Goals... 35

Chapter 4 – Profit Models 51

Chapter 5 – Anti-Pricing................................ 91

Chapter 6 – Systems 97

Chapter 7 – Teams 121

Chapter 8 – Support...................................... 139

Chapter 9 – Breakthrough Action................ 149

Appendixes 160

I want to acknowledge the friends, teachers and mentors who have opened my eyes, held out guiding hands, gleefully tossed Breakthrough ideas into my lap and made this life one heck of an adventure. I would not be where I am today, nor would this book have come to fruition without their presence in my life.

Millie Flateau for showing me what a change of environment can do to create a shift in perspective; Rabbi Dov Berkowitz for saying "You ask *great* questions"; Ruth Bridger for teaching me to give people nineteen chances instead of one; Audrey Finci for modeling what unbiased input looks like; Harry Palmer for showing the world that Breakthroughs can come from mind-boggling residence in isolation tanks; Tony Robbins for demonstrating "synthesis"; Jennifer Butler for introducing me to new aspects of myself, colleagues and friends of the heart for sharing the journey through laughter, support, exploration, insights and inspiration along the way: Joe Finci, Shirley Komoto, Kathryn Tralli, Sheldon Chad, Limor Schafman, Martin Howey, Sonya Shelton, Joel Bauer, and Stevi Sullivan.

Thanks to the creators of labyrinths around the world that provide perspective-changing walks for my inner and outer worlds, and to all my clients and students whose feedback has helped select and shape the tools I teach, many of which I share with you here.

Special Thanks to James Malinchak who at long last liberated me from my stall out over language and figured out that while I cut through the fog, crap, distractions and BS that have other people stalled, using a different "B" word – Breakthrough – fit beautifully so I could get on with it and finish the darned book.

Finally, extra-special thanks to my friend JoAnn Braheny who edited this book, for understanding that it's neither an academic tome, business report, nor a blog, but is a conversation in writing to give encouragement to entrepreneurs and business owners perched at the edge of their 18-foot high dive platform.

This book is dedicated to
My Two Fathers

Morton Feinholz & Stanley Abrams

With love and thanks for the tools
you each gifted me with that I use
daily on my journey.

"It's what you learn after
you think you know it all
that counts."

~ John Wooden

"When I let go of what I am,
I become what I might be."

~ Lao Tzu

"The key to sustaining
Breakthroughs in your life
Is to make them your
'New Normal.'"

~ Linda Feinholz

INTRODUCTION

This book is about success, in business and in life, and a little known element at the center of huge leaps toward that success. It's one of those topics hinted at in self-actualization circles, in boardrooms of the Fortune 50 companies, and in the halls (or foosball rooms) of fast-growing entrepreneurial companies.

I call them "Breakthroughs" – the act of shifting from what you currently know and believe and see possible to a previously unseen fresh view.

We're all waiting and hoping for "Breakthroughs." The people running those companies all know perfectly well there is no such thing as the 'magic bullet' or the 'red pill' that would create instant results. If it existed you can bet it would be well known by now. Marketing geniuses would be putting it in front of us at every turn. I'd be in line for it, and so would you.

Of course, we can continue to hope and dream such a miraculous tool will show up out of one of the biomedical labs, or high-tech creations happening worldwide.

Until that fantasy becomes real, what we do know is that in business (and life) there are specific activities that breed success: everything from planning, managing, leading, to executing tasks with excellence. No shortcuts there. Building blocks. Road-tested, effective ways to do 'high value' activities that are learnable and transferable. It's what sorts out the good businesses from the failing ones.

While *good* companies are chugging along, sweating through each day, breakthrough-creating tools are being used by 'out-of-the-box' thinkers and builders of *great* businesses to trigger their leaps beyond the good ones. Rather than hang around waiting for insights, ideas and breakthroughs with a little 'b' these courageous folks are deliberately creating the circumstances to trigger quantum leap Breakthroughs with a capital 'B' – the ones that transform minds, decisions, actions and results.

Notice that I said 'the circumstances.' It's as much of a romantic notion that we can create Breakthroughs on call, at a whim, as that there's a red pill that will trigger them 20-minutes after ingestion.

What you can implement now is a series of proven techniques that can help you open the gateway to make enormous leaps forward rather than tiny incremental progress.

These techniques are the time-tested exercises and principles that guide High Payoff thought and action. Not only have I experienced their results personally, executives, entrepreneurs and business owners I've taught them to have launched their own unique transformations using them for more than 20 years.

I'm going to share the keys to harnessing these systematic steps and tools so that you can accelerate the speed and frequency of making Breakthroughs in each area of business.

This system of Breakthrough building blocks can revolutionize both your company and your life.

How do I know that these methods work? Firstly, I've used them in business and in life for years. So have my coaching and consulting clients. Repeatedly.

The material you'll find in this book is the result of thousands of hours I've spent with thought leaders looking for the most effective, efficient and easiest tools and approaches.

Over time I stripped out the superfluous steps learned for myself in hundreds of hours of courses research and study and testing, and used them with the thousands of business people whose case studies you'll get a taste of in the following pages. As I received feedback, I distilled and organized the various elements into The Business Breakthrough System that I use in my consulting and coaching and released as a self-paced program. Again, the users reported that they reliably created their own Breakthroughs, faster and easier than other options they tried. All of that constant research, testing, sorting, sifting and adjusting means that you have access to the refined information that works, if you use it.

Having seen, read, heard and considered thousands of hours and pages of material and real world examples, I can confidently tell you that

**"Breakthroughs are waiting
just one thought away."**

~ Linda Feinholz

It's important that you recognize the source of all Breakthroughs is in Thought. It's only following the thought itself that deeper exploration of the idea, the practicalities of it, the mechanics of new relationships and fresh action can produce actual results. So the first key is to **create the conditions for your Breakthroughs.**

At times those conditions resemble the ones found in personal development and self-actualization programs – those courses and writings that are the result of thousands of years of human endeavors and seeking for enlightenment. So they're time-tested approaches to triggering shifts in thought and action

After all, life and business are merely the actualization of our personal enlightenment, goals, and activated intentions. But enough of the 'woo woo' – here's the practical. Transformation is a 2-stage process. Your willingness to focus attention on these ideas, stories and technique triggers, rather than in your highly trained analytical and critical mind, is the first step.

The second key is to **make the commitment to Action** – discipline and commitment in using them and in following through once you have your Breakthrough. You can think of it as the two keys represented in this arrow:

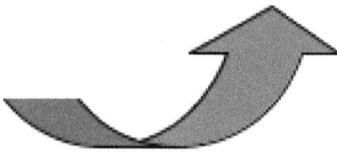

First you sink into the place where you have your insights, then you rise into action to realize the Breakthrough.

You'll find the writing is deliberately fast paced and direct.

Any one idea or sentence can produce "Ah Ha!"s you've been waiting for… if you let them in, let yourself perceive them.

The bottom line is that your building successful results on the spark effect of your Breakthroughs depends on *you* installing new habits, having the new ideas, taking new actions and repeating the cycle again and again.

The purpose of this book is two-fold: to trigger those thoughts for you – to create the first key, the conditions for your Breakthroughs; and to apply those Breakthroughs to the **5 Core Breakdowns** I see most often:

1. Your Team is "busy," but the business is inefficient, ineffective, unprofitable... because they are missing a clear Vision and Goals to anchor all their decisions and activities

2. You're "selling" but your ideal customer isn't buying... because you're more devoted to selling what you want them to buy rather than solutions to what they want solved.

3. Activities that should be reliable and repeatable need too much attention... because you're missing systems that would get it all done with excellence no matter who does it.

4. You're spending too much time training nice smart new hires... because you aren't hiring the highest level of skills and experience which is available and could take your business up to the next level.

5. You're using habitual attitudes and ways of viewing the world, making-decisions, leading and managing... because you don't have fresh ideas, independent support, unbiased feedback and access to new tools and skills so that you can take yourself to your next level.

Solving those breakdowns starts here, now, with the time-proven 5 Core Principles of Breakthroughs.

THE FIVE CORE PRINCIPLES OF BREAKTHROUGHS

1 - SHIFT HAPPENS...
WHEN YOU SEE, FEEL, AND KNOW
WHERE YOU'RE HEADING AND WHY YOU WANT IT

2 - INSIGHT SHOWS UP...
WHEN YOU LET GO OF HOW YOU DO IT NOW

3 - RESULTS ARE EASY...
WHEN YOU DESIGN EVERY ACTIVITY
TO ACHIEVE THEM

4 - CHALLENGES MELT AWAY...
WHEN YOU SURROUND YOURSELF WITH SUCCESS
TEAMS, MODELS AND MENTORS

5 - YOU'LL BREAK THROUGH AGAIN...
WHEN YOU SYSTEMIZE TAKING ACTION ON THEM AND
CELEBRATE THE ONE YOU JUST MADE

This book is designed to give you 9,743 opportunities to have insights, Breakthroughs, and new tools to use to move from Thought to Action. Ready to make Breakthroughs your "New Normal?" Learn these Five Principles and let's get started!

ONE
ONE
ONE

MINDSET

The Greek King Sisyphus was compelled to push a giant boulder up hill, only to watch it roll back down to the bottom, and repeat it throughout eternity. My client **Susan** sat across from me explaining at length how the results she was getting in her business were aggravating and dissatisfying - the same as before. She was shifting constantly in her seat, leaning forward, anxious whether I was buying her reasoning and stories.

It was the fourth time during our work together on her marketing strategies business that she'd come back to a litany of her complaints, the reasons why her current life, results, and reality didn't match what she had planned for herself and her business by this point in her life.

2 | BREAKTHROUGH

As with the three times before, when I asked her what she was ready to change, her answer was to avoid answering and point to outside circumstances - the economy, changes in her industry, challenges with her partner, the lack of accountability in her team, not having the support she needed…

Each time we approached the core – any aspects *within* her control that needed to shift, she had deflected our conversations. She avoided looking at her skills, priorities, decision-making, action in time and productivity, offerings to her customers, leadership and management of her team, support system.

I held up my hand and stopped the stream of discontent and asked her:

"What if it were EASY to make a Breakthrough?"

Letting that sit in the pause for a moment, I then added "Would you use the tools that highly successful people use to accomplish their Visions, create the business they love getting out of bed for on Tuesday Mornings, and have a life they love?

She was utterly silent for two minutes.

I let the silence stretch.

Silence can be oh so uncomfortable and we've all been trained to leap in and fill it rather that let it sit. To let the unspoken find its voice. This time she looked inside for a truthful answer.

This time she got centered, quiet, looked me dead in the eye.

This time she reached Stage 1 of making a Breakthrough.

This time she shifted – her body relaxed, her face relaxed.

In over 20 years of working with folks just like Susan I've

come to recognize the sign of a true Breakthrough approaching:

The stillness and silence are the first signal.

WHY?

Because… we live in a society that has taught us there is honor in business in jumping to immediate answers, in toughing things out, being in action… So if we see ourselves doing those successful actions, why would we act to change them?

Because… we were raised by people who disregarded our dreams and aptitudes and steered us towards what we "ought to do" to fit into a mold at school, in our culture, or in our work.

Because… we are rewarded for having such a high pain tolerance that we deflect any messages our mind and intuition are trying to offer to us, often for decades.

It's only when we actively silence the chatter and create the openness that *allows* us to hear the quiet voice inside… then the outer world fades away along with all our excuses and rationalizations. At last we're ready to perceive something new, to shift, to change, to alter our mindset, so we can see and take the actions that produce the results we really want.

There are plenty of paths to creating silence… but silence does not guarantee openness to Breakthroughs.

SHIFT HAPPENS IN AN INSTANT

In every instance where my students and clients have made the leap from "what has been" into their new way of seeing what they can and what they "will," it's the result of DECIDING to release how they've operated "on automatic," how they "assumed" things must be because of what had been their experience before - how they "argued for their limitations" and won.

It's as if each synapse in their mind unlatches from its former linkages and quickly and simply rearranges itself.

And an entire Universe of new possibilities, new options, new Self, leap into existence and simply 'are.'

I can describe it for you because not only have they experienced that shift, but so have I.

If there truly were a 'pill' I could offer you that created instant shift, perfectly timed enlightenment and complete re-wiring of how you operate in the world, I'd be marketing that to you right now. It doesn't exist.

What does exist is a series of conditions, conversations and new consideration, a system that has produced the highly profitable and successful shifts for hundreds, make that thousands, of people before you.

This system is the roadmap I use when I'm working with my private clients, guiding them through the transformation of their businesses and their lives.

It's the first Building Block for the mastermind groups and online programs I lead with groups of entrepreneurs and business owners - those who have had enough of the way they've been operating – the "hard way" – and want a forum for breaking through their challenges to learn new skills to grow their businesses further, faster, and *easier*.

The result of using 100's of techniques with 1000's of people, road-tested for the ability to create both mindset opening and action follow through, the system is the same one I use for myself when I reach the point where I too want a Breakthrough.

It's composed of 5 core areas of focus:

Breakthrough Visioning & Goal Setting

Defining the focus and anchors for all your time, attention and energy, and that of others on your team to keep all your efforts on track

Breakthrough Profit Models

Designing highly profitable products and services as the perfect solutions for your ideal clients from your experience, expertise and interests

Breakthrough Systems

Deploying ways of working that ensure each and every activity is reliable and repeatable and done with excellence no matter who does it

Breakthrough Teams

Delegating to others who have the skills and ability to become your high performers so you can use your time on the things that require it most

Breakthrough Skills & Support

Developing a strong support foundation for yourself by continuously learning the skills and tools to be the *Leader* of your success through informational programs, and from unbiased advisors, accountability partners

This is the same framework built into my on-line self-paced courses at www.BreakthroughByDesign.com, and shared in the Breakthrough Gold Program and The Breakthrough Academy.

Each of those topics were exactly the ones that Susan had been dodging facing and solving.

And until she was ready to sit in the silence and let her true desires speak up she couldn't experience her first Breakthrough.

Not a shift in the outer world and its results, but inside.

Stop reading. Just let that sink in for a moment.

ALLOW BREAKTHROUGH INSIGHTS

Susan's first shift came when she sent her "this is how it IS" beliefs on vacation for a while so that she could take off the old filters and see fresh visions of the success she'd like to create for herself and the reasons *why* she wanted it.

Without that anchoring, every next thought can be just as attractive as any one before it – each new opportunity can seem just as inviting – each new example of someone else's actions can look like yet another path to try on for ourselves.

We all run into this pattern of chasing bright shiny objects. So we become completely stalled, very busy with activities that have nothing to do with accomplishing our own goals. And then we forget we had goals and become swamped in activity that seems to have its own reasons for existing.

Seems obvious when you read that, doesn't it?

Yet, I don't want you to think I came to understand it out of some inborn brilliance. It was the result of living in that same pattern for myself. Repeatedly. Each time, until I was fed up and at last had had enough and opened to the 'Breakthrough spark'.

According to other folks who have heard my story, my life has been an unusual one. A moving company's dream client.

I was born in California and moved to Europe at the age of eight when my father was offered a job in Geneva, Switzerland. We assumed we'd live there forever. That ended when my father died from a lingering and painful illness when I was fourteen. It was August and my mother, brother and I moved back to Los Angeles in a week's time so we could register for school.

I landed in a 'normal' US high school, suffering through an unfamiliar 'clique' system, surviving it by becoming one of the renegades who hung out with the other "we're-not-a-clique-Clique" members, grateful that this particular system would only have me for four years. I headed to undergraduate studies in San Diego, followed by work opportunities and grad school in LA, then two years working in New York City, and then back to Los Angeles for a great job. Lots of moving about due to external 'circumstances' until I eventually settled in Los Angeles.

That's the broad brushstrokes. Here is a peak into the guts - If being a 'dis-placed' person can be a recommendation for mastering Breakthroughs, each of those moves reinforced it.

At eight years old..."uprooted and transported" by my family's move to Geneva in the middle of 2nd grade. I found myself sitting in a classroom filled with strangers, staring down at a book about "Monsieur Lapin et Madame Lapine" - swamped in confusion and frustration. If not for the pen and ink drawings on the page I never would have known I was reading a story about rabbits in French. I craved unveiling the meaning in the words… until the day "Breakthrough happened" and I burst through the confusion and mystery, into insight and understanding this new language.

In my teens… listening to conversations of people around me about how they were stuck in the teen dramas of their lives… "Breakthrough happened" when I realized choosing a college to go to was the first step in taking on making choices when confronted with infinite possible pathways.

In my twenties… working summers on the production line of the fast growing start up business of a family friend, I looked at the steps I was using over and over again, and the material I was producing. I casually turned to the owner of the business and asked "Is there any reason we cannot reposition the machinery, which would cut out 30 percent of the production process?" A month later, realizing I was producing reports I'd produced before I asked "Is there a way we can hang on to the original files rather than send them to the client, who keeps losing them?" … and "Breakthrough happened" as I accidentally learned all about "power questions." Yes, Breakthroughs for the Company's bottom line. But also I realized the answers to my 'natural' questions, ones that no one else asked, reduced the effort it took to the entire company to produce industry revolutionizing results, and added 6-figures of profits to their bottom line.

In 1995… working with one of my first 'small' business owner clients, **Nick**, I gave him an assignment of an article to read. At our next meeting he looked at me and said "I don't think I'm the right person to run this company through its next stage." His Breakthrough was he realized it was not his vision, nor his need, to grow his company. And that idea ran counter to everything the business gurus and management consulting stars were touting from stages and authoritative books, all of which were constantly spouting the message "If your business isn't growing, it's dying!" My Breakthrough was "It's about our own Vision and Goals for ourselves, not some guru's ideas to sell books or some University professor's publish-or-perish theory."

BUST THROUGH ASSUMPTIONS

Gurus are wrong. Their generalities completely miss the point – this was Nick's *life*. To live *his* best life he needed to open himself to Breakthrough. When he did, and it allowed us to transform both his business and his life, as you'll see throughout this book.

Each of those Breakthroughs was the result of a mindset shift. If you stay open to them, they'll keep right on coming. One of my own most powerful ones came in 2008.

Tim Ferris took the world by storm with his book, *The 4-hour Week*, sharing his stories of the ways he kept breaking the models of work and life he was surrounded by, all to eliminate 'work' from his life so he could spend his time in other pursuits.

Ironically, his book was published during a period when I had been living 4-hour workweeks for quite a while. Some people envied me creating that life. I left the corporate world for my own independent consulting, loving the flexibility and doubling my income while cutting my 'work' hours by 75%.

Reading Tim's book, letting my mind and imagination play with the examples of other people that he shared, triggered my own next Breakthrough.

I realized that I didn't want 'that' any longer.

For years I had been creating great results with clients, while restless and bored with myself, and not able to share that feeling with people around me who were working "hard" and viewing me as having found freedom.

In fact, in my heart I wanted 'more' …

More activity, with more people, showing them how to take their experience and expertise and turn it into lucrative streams of income for themselves.

More engagement with people turned on by making Breakthroughs in their lives.

More ways to make more, play more, and make more of a contribution to the world.

Until I allowed myself to see those inner longings, to feel how deep my inner struggle was, to stop living inside the story I had constructed about how great my life was… I couldn't make my own next Breakthrough.

Want to know the big secret about Breakthroughs?

Breaking through happens in an instant.

Often we feel completely stalled, cannot even describe what 'different' would look like, but we long for it quietly and relentlessly, deep inside.

In the chapters to follow, we'll be discussing both the inner world Breakthroughs as well as the outer world ones that are critical for you to realize Breakthrough business success.

Why am I focusing on "business?"

Because these are our weekday daylight hours, when we

are using all our intelligence, energy and experience.

Because this is how and when we access our own creativity to make a difference in our lives and the lives of others.

Because you and I both know that it's no secret that things are changing around us today, faster than ever before.

Technology has become more sophisticated, competition more keen, and consumers – the people who buy your products and services – have become more educated and aware.

And what about YOU? Are you changing?

With the wide variety of choices your customers or clients have, not only in similar products and services from different companies, but also in the individual people they deal with, it stands to reason that the more skillful and professional you are at meeting your customer's needs, the bigger advantage you can command, and the more effective and successful you will become.

If you're really going to be effective and successful in the marketplace today, it is necessary, even vital, that you continually change, improve, adjust and update your selling, service, and problem solving skills, as well as your methods of marketing and general business operation.

You're not the first person to wish it were different and want it easier.

Seekers have spent entire lifetimes looking for the perfect solution to their challenges, and come up with the following transferable truths you've no doubt heard.

Truth Number One

> **"We cannot solve our problems with the same thinking we used when we created them."**
>
> **~ Albert Einstein**

If you start every meeting with this thinking, there is every possibility you'll find solutions that are easily understood by everyone, and easily implemented as well.

Truth Number Two

> **"Nobody can go back and start a new beginning, but anyone can start today and make a new ending."**
>
> **~ Maria Robinson**

Many of the executives and business owners I work with start off reluctant to voice or write down their goals. There is some inner sense that it's asking for failure to show up rather than success.

A goal is just anchoring for decision-making and for tracking how closely your actions are getting you those results. If you don't declare where you're aiming, you can't double check if you're on course or awry.

You need that information to figure out what you've achieved and what you're learning.

Your learning will allow you to decide if you have different goals you want to aim for – to reset the 'ending' you are currently working towards.

Truth Number Three

"Believe and act as if it were impossible to fail."
~ Charles F. Kettering

Our brain is wired to experience what we imagine with the same synapses as the ones we experience the outer world's events with. When we take action, our brain perceives those actions as proof of reality.

So if you envision what you want to accomplish, and take action on it, your entire brain aligns to help you make it work out. See an obstacle? That's fine. Now visualize a solution.

What did I learn from my own Breakthroughs?

"Every instance of Breakthrough feels like a unique leap.
~ Linda Feinholz

Unfathomable before the shift, accompanied by a rush of adrenaline and a whoosh as it happens, and leaving a sensation of complete certainty and ease on the other side.

I've become a Breakthrough Junkie, devoted to teaching others how to have them for themselves. And that's what this book is all about. It has been written with the goal of helping *you* become the best you can be at what you do professionally.

Naturally, this book doesn't claim, nor does it pretend, to have all the answers to all your business problems. No book, course or seminar could do that.

Rather, I want to expose you to some tried, tested, and field-proven ideas, concepts, and techniques that have worked for other business people much like you. Four Building blocks that have triggered Breakthroughs in their businesses and their lives.

COURAGE

… to step out of the pack away from what 'everyone else' knows and believes and does…

+

CURIOSITY

… to allow yourself to see what you've never before let yourself see…

+

CONDITIONS

… to create the environment, resources, and the previously unimaginable that can suddenly make perfect sense…

+

COMMITMENT

… to take previously unimaginable actions that can suddenly make perfect sense…

=

BREAKTHROUGH

Think of the process as using a series of states. I call them…

"The 4 C's of BREAKTHROUGHS"

Are you open to trying on these 4 C's?

Once acquainted with new information and ideas, it will then be up to you to decide which ideas can best be tailored to your own individual business situation, and how you will begin to use them to create your business Breakthroughs.

While I share marketing ideas here, the goal of my sharing this information is not to try to make you a marketing expert.

Rather, the purpose is to provide you with some of the tools that marketing experts and those who have created Breakthroughs in business are currently using.

Together, we'll explore specific Breakthrough mindset, skills, business models, marketing, sales, customer service, and business building techniques that others have used to significantly increase their businesses and incomes with very little extra effort.

Obviously this first chapter is all about mindset.

You may be asking yourself "Why is Linda spending so much time on this already?"

Because if we don't get you willing to Pause in the Silence as you read, and open up, there won't be Breakthroughs.

Susan paused in the silence of our meeting.

Nick paused by walking away from his office to read the material I gave him.

It's important to keep an open mind as you read, hear, or

otherwise experience ideas that can help you. Ideas are powerful. And good ideas are really important for any business.

Try not to judge them or cast them aside too quickly because they don't sound good, they're not part of your personality or make up, or because you may have heard them before.

BREAKTHROUGH MINDSET TIP 1

If you've heard an idea before, say to yourself, "Yes, I've heard that before, but am I using it?"

If not, ask "Why not?"

If you are currently using the idea, ask yourself, "How effectively am I at using it?

"How can I 'plus', or improve on it to make it even more effective for me and my business?"

Next, ask yourself this question: "What will I do as a result of what I've learned?"

Here's an example of pushing you to the edge:

* * * * *

You're NOT in the (whatever business you're in) business...

You're in the MARKETING business.

Read those sentences again... and again... and again.

Digest them.

Understand them.

Internalize them.

Make them an integral part of your business philosophy.

Because unless and until you do, your business will be no better and no different than any of the other choices your prospects and customers can select to do business with.

Whether you own your company or work for someone else you're in the Marketing business.

Let me explain by using the insurance profession as an example, and as I do, first think about how these principles might apply to your business.

It's a well-known fact that very few people (if any at all), actually want to buy an insurance policy.

It's true, they may want the benefits, security and peace of mind that insurance provides them and their families or their business, but they don't necessarily want to spend their money on an insurance policy.

But, what do most insurance sales people sell?

They sell insurance!

No wonder the business is so difficult. It doesn't take a Harvard degree to figure it out. If you sell insurance... and know that people don't want to dwell on bad possibilities... why would you keep beating your head against the wall trying to sell fear?

Consider the way most people shop for auto insurance.

They call up a number of insurance companies asking for a quote. The agent or his or her representative asks what coverage the caller is currently carrying, and gives a quote based on those figures. The caller then thanks the agent or staff member, and goes to the next number on their list.

They keep repeating that scenario until they're convinced that they've found the lowest price... and whichever company comes in lowest gets the business.

But, wait a minute.

Isn't there more to buying insurance than just "low price?"

Well, sure there is.

And you and I both know it.

And so do most insurance agents.

Why is it, then, that nearly every agent from nearly every insurance company you call tries to sell on price... knowing that there's probably someone out there with a lower price than they can quote?

Why is it that so few agents try to differentiate themselves from their competition, and change the prospect's base of thinking away from price, and on to other, more important things?

* * * * *

Now let's Pause here for a second. You may find yourself checking out of reading this discussion because I'm using "marketing" or "insurance agent" as the example...

Did you notice yourself mentally skipping over the words "insurance agent" and missing the ideas, the messages in the example itself?

I LOVE using this example to unveil your mindset!

This book is not about being an insurance agent, an employee, an entrepreneur.

It's about making Breakthroughs IN those areas, in whichever profession or discipline you're working. Sparking the 'new' insight or idea.

Who is in charge of your attention? Is it you, your mindset or your emotional resistances to topics and idea?

BREAKTHROUGH MINDSET TIP 2

If you want a Breakthrough in your life, or in your business, you need to notice when 'resistance' creeps in.

Use it as a signal.

Don't let it steer your attention away.

YOU need to own your attention, so that you stick with what is unfamiliar and not have your attention slipping into avoidance and excuse making without your noticing it!

THIS is the realm of Breakthroughs!

There are many ways to access that Shift as Nick and Susan did. The common element is that each of them was ready to let go of the old elements they'd held onto, the very ones that had created their own overwhelm and stall outs.

At some level they'd made the decision to step forward to meet their Breakthroughs.

Susan and I focused our monthly meetings on assumption-busting conversations. Between our meetings she had assignments that had her envisioning, reading, and using ideas to deliberately challenge what had her stuck. Stuck working six and half days a week on multiple businesses.

Once she was ready do the exercises I gave her, she opened to making shifts in her old assumptions and their results.

From stuck for years, to making her first Breakthrough in 17 days, and her third in 3 days, she began to believe she could indeed create a very different path to the results she wanted.

The more often she let herself step into that space, the faster and more often she was able to trigger her own Breakthroughs.

INVITE YOUR BREAKTHROUGHS TO JOIN YOU

Ready to invite your own Breakthroughs to show up?

If you'll come play with me in the opportunities to shift that I bring you throughout the following pages, we'll lay out the 'Welcome' mat to your own future.

On the next page, and following each of the chapters below, I've given you a guide that will let you take the ideas you've just read, and take steps to use them in your own life.

To get the greatest value you can from this material, I recommend you both draft your Action Plan and share it with others.

Find other people who are also on the Breakthrough Path.

By sharing your learning and what you are doing with it you'll be encouraging their support and participation.

Consider these folks your accountability partners who will help you maintain your focus and Breakthrough Mindset.

It all starts with two assignments:

1 – Document your Ah Ha's from this chapter, and

2 – Create a Breakthrough Action Plan.

My Ah Ha's

☐

☐

☐

☐

☐

And now, make it your "New Normal" through using your Breakthrough action plan.

BREAKTHROUGH ACTION PLAN

☐   Select the result you want to have 'different' in your life, in your business

☐   Set aside 15 minutes uninterrupted to focus your thoughts on that idea

☐   List all the things you know about 'why things are the way they are' – your current beliefs – about the way your life or business is now operating

☐   Write down the key obstacles, frustrations or aggravations in each of those areas

☐   Write down your wishes and dreams for each of them

☐   Prioritize the order in which you're willing to examine and shift those items

☐   Share your list with others who you want to have involved

☐   Mark time on the calendar to take on the first one on the list you're ready to challenge

☐   Add all the new assumptions you uncover to your list

NOW create a file where you'll keep your notes and track your results.

TWO

TWO
TWO

VISION

During 2010 I was coaching **Karen** and **Jennifer**, young eager entrepreneurs whose business growth had stalled at $750,000 in revenue for four years. They were completely frustrated by their own "rock of Sisyphus."

Their old approach wasn't working. Jennifer was flying around the world working with personal clients, periodically blogging about the product as Karen was doing all the work of their company, working 80-hour weeks designing product, marketing, organizing trade shows, overseeing web sales with one operations coordinator cum office manager salesman, Mike.

Karen wasn't solving their stall out, just reinforcing her own overwhelm. She and Jennifer couldn't even discuss matters.

Adding a marketing coordinator and an operations coordinator didn't solve the situation because there were no systems and no management activities taking place. Decisions were taking six to nine months to be made because there was no shared vision or goals to guide them.

All three were utterly annoyed with each other every day blaming the others for the non-results. Neither partner could answer my questions "What do you want? What are you trying to do?"

I was reminded yet again that the first step in breaking through is having a "clear Vision" of where you want to go.

WHAT TRIGGERS OUR VISIONS

For myself, my first experience of a Breakthrough Vision was while longing to learn a new language. My second was while trying to escape high school, the third while wanting to get a production process smooth-flowing and easy. The fourth occurred while being frustrated about having to duplicate efforts, and the fifth was while wanting the entire workflow… to flow.

I could 'see' the different futures I wanted.

So what about you? If someone could wave a magic wand and suddenly change something about your chosen profession or business, what one thing would you have them change?

Would you have them provide you with an easier way to contact more, better-qualified prospects? And would you want those prospects as well as your current customers to view you as even more of a professional, or maybe even a "unique expert" in your field?

You may be good now, but how would you like to be even better at making more effective, more persuasive presentations?

Perhaps you'd like to be more effective at closing sales or handling objections. Is repeat business more important to you?

What if your current customers felt that you were the only person or the only business that understood and could effectively serve their specialized, unique and individual needs?

Or, how about referrals? Take the best customer you have right now. How would you like to have more contacts just like him than you could possibly handle?

Would you have them wave that wand to hand you an easier way to design and deliver products, services, information built on your expertise and experience, that your ideal customer has been searching for – and gave up hoping to find?

Would you want those customers to value results you deliver so highly that there is no ceiling on what you could charge?

Your business may be good now, but would you like to be even better at using more effective, more reliable systems and teams?

Perhaps you would like to be more effective at keeping your attention on the High Payoff activities that need your attention while you confidently hand off the rest of what needs to get done to others you can trust will do it, and do it well.

Is bottom-line growth your goal?

Or, is a highly lucrative lifestyle business more important to you?

What if you could get out of bed on Tuesdays with the

confidence that you had all the "know how" you need to run your business perfectly, including a compelling vision, concrete goals, a highly profitable business model, leverage systems, a high performance team, and access to all the advice you need, right when you need it?

What one thing would you change to make you a better, happier, and more productive businessperson?

Stick with the underlying idea here:

It doesn't matter what industry we're referring to.

It doesn't matter what product we're talking about here.

It doesn't matter what service or solution or remedy or transaction (see all the other professions we can cover?).

My clients Susan, Nick, Karen and Jennifer, learned that there isn't a single action you'll take in the outer world, that you'll follow through on over time, if you don't understand the first Principle of Breakthroughs.

BREAKTHROUGH PRINCIPLE 1

SHIFT HAPPENS...
WHEN YOU SEE, FEEL, AND KNOW
WHERE YOU'RE HEADING AND WHY YOU WANT IT

Whether you are starting out, or making your shifts and quantum leaps in an existing business, there are distinct stages and opportunities for Breakthroughs.

There is a specific sequence of Building Blocks to use to grow your business further, faster, easier:

It all starts with creating a compelling Vision.

CASE STUDIES

Nick had been running his $5million company for 10 years, after buying it from his father and his father's business partner. He had focused on sales for the first seven years in the business as he worked for the company as an employee, then he stepped into the ownership role.

His company produced manufacturing equipment and ancillary supplies for manufacturing operations. His products were sold through regional distributors in many different industries. He cleared 17 percent net profit annually. He owned his property and buildings and equipment debt free.

When we first met, Nick had a long list of frustrations with his market, his team, his sense of overwhelm about decision-making for his business.

For our start-up focus he asked for a comprehensive assessment of the business and his team.

While I conducted that evaluation, I also asked him to sort out his goals for the businesses so that we could use both sets of information in determining our next steps.

His immediate answer back to me was "double the size of the business."

I looked at his profit model's results, his systems, his team, his leadership and management practices, and I laid out all the areas we'd systematically improve to create that growth.

As that plan was being developed, with all the implications for how he would need to grow and use new skills and practices, redesign his marketing and sales activities and operations, I asked him to detail his Vision for himself, his family, and again for his business.

He took the assignment seriously.

The next time we met he looked me straight in the eye and said "I have all the money I want for retirement, for all of my children's educations, and for the life my wife and I want. I don't believe I'm the person to run this business if the target is significant growth. Perhaps in a few years my son would want to make that his challenge. For now, I want this business to be easier and more profitable to run."

Clarifying his Vision allowed to us to reset all his goals.

His Vision. His Goals.

"Good business leaders create a vision, articulate the vision, passionately own the vision, and relentlessly drive it to completion."

~ Jack Welch

You'll see the results of that in the chapters below.

My client **Elaine** was stuck on the horns of a dilemma.

She had been making exquisite unique jewelry for wealthy private clients who kept telling her she ought to sell more than just at the trunk shows they held in their homes.

She loved creating her pieces... and she hated the idea of spending her time duplicating them.

She valued each piece's uniqueness. She used systems for making her jewelry that no one else used.

She loved making the connections with her clients, but didn't want to become a salesman hawking them from shop to shop.

For six months she made no headway moving beyond the idea of growing her business, until she and I started to work on what had her stalled.

As the first step, we uncovered her underlying Vision. She intended to apply to a fines-arts masters program in a couple of years. As she put her plans together, she realized she could fund her graduate studies by 'expanding her business' but she couldn't imagine how to do that.

Her next Breakthrough came when she realized she was fine with her pieces being duplicated and sold multiple times, as long as she didn't have to do that duplicating..

Today her pieces are seen on celebrities in the movies, on TV and in fashion magazines, are sold consistently in luxury boutiques and resorts, and available on-line.

Yet none of it could have been sorted out, nor could the work to accomplish it have been sustained, until she could describe her own compelling Vision.

From Vision through designing the elements of her operations, to her marketing activities and pricing. From Vision through Action to Results.

I'll share more of the steps we took in the next few chapters.

In the previous chapter I discussed my client **Susan**.

Rather than a products business, Susan was in the 'services' industry. She viewed her services as highly expert, yet kept positioning them so they were viewed as expensive commodities.

Until Susan's own Breakthrough, shifting to view herself as more insightful and more strategic than her competitors, she was unable to change her message about the results she obtained for her clients.

And without different messaging, her prospective customers kept lumping her in with 'everyone else' in her industry.

When she did the Visioning exercises and had her Breakthrough she was able to see herself and her results as materially different than other service providers. And she was able to design language to describe it in a way that her clients knew, the moment they read her marketing or heard her speak, that she was "exactly what they needed."

BACK TO YOU

You'll see throughout the case studies I include for you that there are Breakthroughs that can happen in every aspect of your business. They may be for you individually or for your entire team.

The underpinning of all of this is to focus systematically on how you approach creating changes in your business, so that you live those weekday daylight hours more productively and more pleasurably while creating a lucrative income stream that allows you to create a life you love living.

How you live life becomes your 'habits'.

Just like the way we brush our teeth every day, most of our thinking, our conversations, our responses to other people are firmly rooted habits. New results require new habits.

Not single-use new behaviors, but Breakthrough changes to your habits that you stick with for the long term. But here's the reality you've already experienced hundreds of times in your own life – habits are hard to change.

New behaviors don't stick unless you *value* making the change from how you're on automatic now… UNTIL you have a Vision that is MORE COMPELLING than your old habits.

Don't think that sitting staring out the window for ten minutes, imagining a great vacation, is enough to anchor a change. So many people enter into business and spend years in that business environment without having any idea of what they want, or what is possible to get out of their business. For that reason I have eight different visioning exercises I take my clients through in order to uncover and define their Vision.

It's no different in large corporations, in entrepreneurial endeavors, or in the legal or insurance profession. In fact, most business owners are working so hard in their businesses that they don't have time to work 'on' them. As a result, they've become slaves to their business.

They've got things backwards. They're working for their business rather than their business working for them.

Are you?

The whole point of creating your Breakthrough Vision is to know yourself and exactly what you want in life AND therefore what you're willing to put 'in' and expect 'out' of your business.

Typically people don't even want to begin Visioning, fearing it will lead them to see some notions they've deliberately kept concealed from themselves, layered in their imagination with assumptions about what they might 'have to' do if they see it.

Yet once you see your Vision you'll feel liberated, enlivened, and see a path forward. And when you share it with others, your family and team, they too will be able to bring their hearts and passion and best work to make it come true too.

So take the time to…

DEFINE a clear VISION for yourself, one that inspires you daily, and turn it into goals that let you know you're achieving it.

It's the first step to calming your overwhelm and releasing the brake on what has held you stuck for too long.

It's the access point to the inner conversation with the wise inner truths you've been carrying with you and pushing off – out of sight and out of mind – divorcing yourself from your own uniqueness. NOW declare what will fulfill you instead!

It's your opportunity to hand yourself your own golden ticket to the ride you'd rather be taking in this lifetime.

It's how you'll be living your life and it all starts with a shift, a Breakthrough Vision, so we can move you on to your goals.

So find a quiet, undistracted location and open up your mind.

Do it on your own, with music playing or silence, with pen and paper nearby at hand, or do it with the Visioning exercises you'll find at www.BreakthroughByDesign.com and two weeks from today you're going to have a clear Vision for the next stage of your business and life, one that has you leaping out of bed eagerly on Tuesdays for the sheer pleasure of the day you'll be living.

My Ah Ha's

☐

☐

☐

☐

☐

Pick one aspect of your current business and use the

Breakthrough Action Plan.

BREAKTHROUGH ACTION PLAN

- ☐ Select the new aspect of your business you want to take on
- ☐ Set aside 15 minutes uninterrupted
- ☐ Visualize a new result you want, and the way through taking the Action
- ☐ See the tools, resources, information you need, and organize them
- ☐ Put it on the calendar
- ☐ Share it with others whom you want to have involved
- ☐ Mark time on the calendar to review how it went after you've taken the action
- ☐ Decide how you'll adapt it and use it again

For a taste of guided Visioning exercises, be sure to visit www.BreakthroughByDesign.com

As circumstances change and your Vision is accomplished, when life changes and your intentions change, you'll refresh your Vision again. Then make that your "New Normal."

THREE
THREE
THREE

GOALS

Some time back a mentor of mine had the opportunity of having dinner with his friend Earl Nightingale, the famous radio personality and producer of recorded self-improvement programs – a man he admired highly and was thrilled to meet in person.

Earl made his life's work studying successful people and how they achieved their successes. My friend had long admired Earl for his ideas and philosophy. And on that occasion, my friend asked him what advice he would pass on to his young son if he had one.

What, based on Earl's vast experience and knowledge, would be the one thing that would help his son ensure success both in business as well as in his personal life.

Earl said told him, "You know, I have often thought about that very question.

"And after all the years and all the study, I've come to the conclusion that your success in life, or in business for that matter, can be boiled down to one thing.

"That is, your rewards will always be in direct proportion to the amount of service you render.

"You only have to look around," he said.

"The people who serve others prosper. The people who don't serve others don't prosper. And you can tell just how successful a person is by the amount of service they render to others.

"The problem," he continued, "is that unsuccessful people either haven't learned that great secret, or they don't apply it.

"The successful people are the ones who develop the habits of doing the things that unsuccessful people don't do for one reason or another."

Now for a moment, I'd like you to imagine that it's a Tuesday morning, you're sitting at your desk facing a long To Do list.

Got the picture?

What is it that gets you into action when that list is sitting there in front of you?

For my clients and course members, and me too, it takes one fundamental grounding point to get our attention and energy focused, inspired and into action. That is recognizing how our time and energy and attention are serving others. And how the results of our service to others will help us create a life we want to live.

But here's a trick that gets left out of the conversation about 'service'. Vision isn't enough.

On a grand scale, for lack of a Vision, we spend our days in motion without direction. Without Goals there is no progress in achieving a Vision in and of itself.

FROM VISIONS TO FOCUSED ACTION

Vision, ideas and strategies alone, won't create results. You've got to take action on them, if you expect anything different than what you're currently getting.

And that Action needs to have a purpose – creating a result, both for yourself and particularly for others – a service it's delivering. That means laying out Goals towards achieving the Vision.

For lack of Goals, we each get pulled off focus, day in and day out. Our attention gets snagged by distractions, so we don't think things through to completion and take effective action on them in a timely manner.

The breakdowns get even worse as they're magnified by the size of the company and team.

If no one on your team knows what goals they ALL should be working towards, every decision takes four times as long as it needs to, and often they aren't even heading in the same direction.

Your team starts chasing any bright shiny new idea that comes along.

So you get overwhelmed and stalled. And they spin their wheels day after day.

I could go on and on, but you get the picture.

It sure makes for Tuesdays that feel like failures, doesn't it?

Earl's comments hit my mentor like a big hammer that night, as he realized how true they were.

The more you serve your customers, and help them satisfy *their* goals, the more you will prosper.

And as a business owner, business manager, professional person or entrepreneur, serving your customer's needs effectively means that you must DO the things that unsuccessful business owners, managers, professionals, and entrepreneurs don't do.

The things that those unsuccessful people don't do are the things that most of us don't like to do either.

WHAT FAILURES DON'T LIKE TO DO

One of the things most people avoid doing is setting Goals.

That means goals for themselves AND goals for the results they'll create for their customers.

Why? Because we've been trained to pay attention to what we *failed* to accomplish, our shortcomings, rather than what we've achieved.

Neither in school nor in business are we asked "What did you learn this far? How will you use it next? What else will you add next?" Instead we're asked "What did you miss?"

So if you never write down a Goal, no one will ask you "So,

how's it going getting that accomplished?"

There is no doubt that it is difficult to work long hours or on weekends when your family is waiting for you at home, and only have a couple of "shoppers" stop by or be stood up for an appointment someone made with you.

It's tough to make telephone calls, only to be met with hostile and rude people on the other end who curse at you or slam the phone down.

It's discouraging to set goals, schedule interviews, explain the technical aspects and benefits of the products and services you provide, overcome customer's objections and misconceptions, and go out of your way to give exceptional service, only to have your customer go elsewhere because they found the same product or service for a few dollars less.

Enough of these experiences can be discouraging for anyone. And after a while, some people just quit trying.

They find it easier to adjust their standard of living downward to match their income, than to adjust their income upward to create their desired standard of living.

They are no longer in control. Inflation dictates the price of things they buy, and competition and luck determine how much they have to spend. Fortunately for them, many of their competitors are in the same situation... so everyone's results are stalled.

Outstanding success is unusual, and is dependent on many different factors. For some people, it just happens. Most of the time they're in the right place at the right time, doing nothing special, everything just 'falls into place' for them. Others put in long hours and much work, only to find they've created just average success.

SEPARATE YOURSELF FROM THE PACK

A clear Vision that inspires you daily gets you out of bed enthusiastically is a critical Building Block. Your Breakthrough Vision is the starting point. If you don't know where you want to go, you'll have no idea of what to do in order to get there. And you won't follow through even if you do have an 'idea.'

You need those 'before' and 'after' images clearly in mind because you need to make that Vision practical, observable, describable to others so they can help get it achieved.

The next Building Block is identifying how you'll recognize if your time, attention and energy are getting you to that Vision.

Roald Amundsen and Robert Falcon Scott each held a vision of getting their team "first" to the South Pole. Scott focused on madly racing and his entire team died. Amundsen focused on 20 miles a day, made it and brought his team home alive.

You've got to convert your attention from the reverie of Visioning to the Actions you'll take in your current world in order to achieve that Vision. So the immediate ACTION to take after defining your Vision is to convert it into Goals.

Keep in mind, it's not just in the corporate world where our habits keep us stalled. A funny thing happens when you hang out in the world of self-actualization and human potential programs.

All too often people leave the retreats and seminars pumped up full of enthusiasm and a sensation of expansion and possibility. It's often someone else's vision, not yours, that you hold. AND there is no true desire for it so no goals are set and acted upon. Six months later? Perhaps you've got insights and know how, but no measurable difference in your life.

So, deep inside the anxiety and churn continues.

Outside, the overwhelm and stall out and frustration that you're not making any headway keeps chewing at you.

What's missing in many of development programs, even if you uncover your own personal Vision, is the action of turning the Vision into real world practical observable Goals.

For the lack of a goal no plan is made …

For the lack of a plan no action is taken …

For the lack of action no result is made …

So no Vision makes it out from behind the habits of our thoughts and behavior into the world.

To create the conditions that create Breakthrough Results, after we craft a Vision that inspires us AND share it with others so they can be inspired and support our achieving it…

It's time to turn it into a list of real world steps we'll take to move from where we are today towards that specific Vision.

That means making the commitment to converting Visions into Goals so that you'll follow through in action: doing what ever it takes to find the information, tools, resources and relationships that will break through the fog that keeps us stuck in "How Things Work Now."

Into the light of "How We'll Get Things Done NEW."

GOALS ARE VISIONS MADE PRACTICAL

Breakthrough goals are an essential requirement for success

in business. With goals, you have a target to aim for, a purpose for being, and a direction to travel. And this applies to everyone on your team.

Without goals, it's easy to wander aimlessly, getting sidetracked with any inspiring new thing that comes along.

With Goals, you have a target to use as you select actions that will make it 'inevitable' that you'll accomplish those Goals.

When you set your goals, think of the word, "SMART" You should test each goal you set on the following five criteria.

BREAKTHROUGH GOALS TIP 1

Your Goals Should Be S.M.A.R.T.

**Specific – Measurable – Achievable
Realistic – Time-bound**

It is important for your goals to be Specific, so you will know exactly what you're aiming for.

Your goal should be clearly defined and identified so you not only know what you are trying to accomplish, you'll also know when you attain it. And so will the rest of your team.

Saying you want to help more people, sell more products, merchandise or services or reduce the number of contacts to close a sale isn't enough.

You need to specify your goal clearly. Is it 30 more clients,

12 more sales per month? An extra $100,000 in monthly sales? How about a certain amount of certain types of products or services?

How much – *specifically*?

Whatever your goal, there should be no doubt about what you wish to accomplish.

Your goals should be Measurable.

That is, there should be a system, or method of determining how you are progressing in your efforts for attainment.

By clearly defining your goals as discussed in the previous step, you will be more able to measure them. It's important for you to be able to see your current status, as well as progression towards your goals.

Next, your goals should be Attainable. If your goal is too high… if there's no hope for you to reach it, it won't take long for you to become discouraged, and you will either lose concentration and the drive necessary to pursue your goal, or you will abandon it altogether.

Your goal should be something you can reach with just a little extra effort.

OUT OF THE BOX AND A BIT OF A STRETCH

An insurance agency owner I'm acquainted with had a large fire and casualty agency. In order to promote the sale of life insurance to his on-board customers, the agency owner introduced a contest for his agents. The agent who sold the most life insurance would win a trip to Hawaii.

One of the agents who worked for the agency but who had

never sold much life insurance, decided he wanted to try and win the trip. The qualifications to earn the trip were tough, and were based entirely on the sale of life insurance.

Very few agents in this agency ever earned these types of trips by working the entire year for them, but this particular agent put his mind to it and qualified in only four months.

Considering the agent's past performance with regards to life insurance sales, you might question whether the goal should have been attainable for him. However, the agent found a motivation within that changed the odds to his favor, and he was able to accomplish in a four-month period, what most agents weren't able to do in an entire year.

In your business operation, you need to make sure your goals are not only attainable, but are also... Realistic. If your goal isn't realistic, that is, if it's not something within your realm of achievement, it's just a matter of time before you'll become frustrated and give up.

And that can have a negative effect on you as you begin to think of yourself as a failure, or not being good at setting goals.

Then, because of your negative image of yourself relative to setting goals, you will likely give up setting goals in the future.

It's a self-feeding mechanism.

The key to being good at setting and achieving goals is to be realistic in your expectations. Set attainable and realistic goals that can be reached with a small amount of effort.

That builds a success image, and enhances your self-confidence in a positive way.

Then, the next time, set a little higher goal. Not much higher, just a little higher.

Again, select goals that you know you can achieve. And ones that will build your confidence that much more.

The next step is to make your goals Time-bound.

That is, you should set a time limit for their attainment and for the periods during which you give them your attention. Is 30-days the right span? 3 months? 180 days? 2 Years?

This helps you keep on target, not be distracted, and encourages you to complete something you've started.

"What you get by achieving your goals is as important as what you become by achieving your goals."

~ Henry David

Not only will this help you to realize success at a pre-designated time, but you will enhance your self image by accomplishing your goal.

If, for instance, your goal is to sell a certain number of a certain type of product or service, or a pre determined dollar amount of sales this year, break that number down into months, weeks, and even days, if necessary. A large goal becomes much more manageable in small pieces.

The key is to break your goals into bite size pieces, and place a time deadline on them, for their accomplishment.

CASE STUDIES

My client **Paul** sent me an email declaring "My calendar is full! Fabulous!"

Seems perhaps like the opposite of what you might want yours to look like?

In fact his business model had long lead times for sales of his services, high-end consulting to mega-corporations that could take eighteen months or more. Then his engagements would consist of entire days or weeks of time booked at individual clients.

So when he looked at his calendar much of it was 'empty.'

And empty felt discouraging for him, regardless of what his revenue looked like over the span of a year or two.

By developing a broader Vision for himself, he added Goals for how he would use his time developing articles, books, and speeches. Then he scheduled all those activities into time blocks each week so that when he looked at his calendar he had distinct activities he knew he would spend his time on.

And he loved seeing a calendar that was 'booked' with more than the networking meetings and periodic client development time that had been there already.

Here's a perfect example of the exact opposite Goal: My client **Darren** was running a $100 million manufacturing business's operation. Every day he started with a full calendar - all the meetings with other key managers in the business, with outside vendors and with key customers.

And at the end of each day, when he looked up at his white

board where he had written the top six most critical strategic issues that needed his attention, he had not spent even five minutes on any of them. He couldn't carve out the time to do the Visioning for each of them, let alone get action taken.

That was until we devoted 90-minutes to focusing in on his Vision for the company - the specifics of what it could be if those strategies were accomplished.

"If you have more than three priorities then you don't have any." ~ Jim Collins

With that clarity in front of him, we were able to look at every single appointment on his calendar, reassign 73% of them to his direct reports, add back short meetings to make sure those were getting taken care of, and then block off on his calendar 30 hours a week to spend solely on those strategies.

The results: Darren took key issues that had been 'back-burnered' for 18 months and got strategic decisions made in 45 days. Moreover, he took his first week-long vacation with his family in seven years without giving a thought to what was going on at the office, nor in his email or voicemails.

Remember **Elaine**, the jewelry designer? Once she set her Vision of funding her next design degree, we were able to calculate living expense goals until then, what it would cost to cover the entire program, relocation, materials, and savings she would want set aside before, during and following the program.

With those Goals in mind we could start designing the business model that would achieve them.

Tamara, one of the members of my Mastermind program, described clearly that she wanted to grow her business exponentially so that it would fund her entire family moving to France.

Her Vision and the Goals associated with it were so clear that we could dive right in to redesigning her Breakthrough Profit Model reshaping it from periodic counseling sessions with women unleashing all of their potential to high priced lifestyle redesign programs in a business that combined self-study information products with ultra high end private programs.

Nick had always been completely resistant to setting goals. In my initial meetings with him he sat with a yellow pad of paper and a sharpened pencil on the desk between us. While I took copious notes from our conversations, his pages remained blank. When I asked him to jot down the answers to questions, the pencil barely left any lead on the page.

With a lot of coaching and sympathy to his resistance I was able to talk him through a fresh look at his manufacturing business, the state of the economy and technology developments in the various industries he served. Once he'd allowed himself to describe his Vision, he was ready to look at setting goals.

By climbing into his sales data for the past several years he was able to look at specific areas he'd like to grow the business, and decide "by how much, by when" for each of his products.

Then we stepped back and took a bird's eye view of what it would take to achieve those results. We brought the entire management team together to review Nick's thinking and priorities, making their suggestions and recommendations and adding their ideas to the mix.

By the end of this process, Nick's goals were transformed from throwing a dart at the wall to his Top 3 SMART goals for the coming year goals the entire Team was vested in accomplishing.

BACK TO YOU

In the previous chapter we talked about how critical it is to have a compelling Vision to keep you motivated in taking on the Breakthrough changes in action to construct new ones. Now it's time for Goal Setting.

My Ah Ha's

- ☐
- ☐
- ☐
- ☐
- ☐

Take the time to carefully analyze where you've come from, where you are now, and what you want to accomplish in your life, including your business, your job or your career. I know it personally and I've got about 78,000 other folks who can testify to the fact that all the techniques in the world are useless if you don't create a compelling reason for your follow through actions.

BREAKTHROUGH ACTION PLAN

- ☐ Select one aspect of your Vision you want to make practical

- ☐ Set aside 15 minutes uninterrupted

- ☐ Convert it into SMART Goals

- ☐ Specify how you'll measure if you're succeeding

- ☐ Review the tools, resources, information you need, and organize them

- ☐ Prioritize which ones you'll work on in what order. Put it on the calendar so you follow through on each one

- ☐ Mark time on the calendar to review how it went after you've taken the action

- ☐ Share it with others who you want to have involved

For a taste of guided Goal Setting exercises, be sure to visit www.BreakthroughByDesign.com/gold

FOUR FOUR FOUR

PROFIT MODELS

May I let you in on a secret? It's not "all about you."

Your business profitability depends entirely on your matching the Vision your ideal clients hold for the thing *they* want solved AND who they believe can solve it.

Most people in 'business' are selling the product or service they personally crave seeing out there in the world. Those entrepreneurs and business owners are missing the point. People don't buy what someone else wants to sell to them. They buy solutions that move them toward their own Visions and Goals from whoever is offering the closest fit. Even unexpected solutions.

I suppose I could have written an entire book on this topic alone, but I prefer to give it to you here in the context of all of the Breakthrough Building Blocks.

As you read this, **take your time**. Explore every one of the tips as your opportunity to open up to the Breakthrough possible for your own business. Take each of the Breakthrough Profit Model Tips I use with my clients and program members and make them your own.

For instance, as a business person, it is important for you to understand that only 35% of the reason people buy the products or services you offer, is for the actual product or service itself.

The other 65% of the reason they buy is for what *you* can do or provide for them beyond the product or service, and what that product or service does for their achieving their own Goals.

What they "need" right now isn't always what they want.

BREAKTHROUGH PROFIT MODEL TIP 1

Everyone lives by WIIFM – "What's In It For Me." Your customers want their issues solved, not your solution.

In other words, if you are trying to sell 'at' your customers and prospects products and services, you are wasting your time.

They are only 35% interested in products and services. But they are 65% interested in the *benefits* of having you involved.

You see chances are good that your customers and prospects can buy the same product or service (or at least comparable ones) from any one of several of your competitors.

And with that product or service, your competitor may offer a number of additional advantages, as well.

They may have a lower price, better quality product, some added bonuses or extra services, a location that's more convenient, or a payment plan that fits their customer's budget better.

In today's tough, competitive market, it's difficult to compete on price or product. Even in the new technology arena.

You may be able to command a certain advantage for a period of time because you have a lower price than your competitors, but you and I both know that it will be short-lived.

The truth is, you will never be able to maintain a competitive position in the marketplace – long-term for any length of time – just because of the prices you charge or the products you provide.

It'll just be a matter of time before either one of your competitors lowers their prices or duplicates (or even betters) your product, or you raise your prices because you no longer have the necessary margins to justify your prices.

But there's one thing your customers can't get from any of your competitors. And that's you, and the empathy, the problem solving expertise and the knowledge, education and commitment to service that you bring to his or her specific and unique situation.

They want someone they can trust.

The fastest path to Breakthrough success is to provide the very thing your customers can't get from any of your competitors. That's the solution that perfectly matches what they're looking for.

BREAKTHROUGH PROFIT MODEL TIP 2

ASK What Your Customers Really Want.

Then they'll hold out their hand and say "I've been looking for YOU!" and you'll add an extra "0" to the revenue you bring in by matching your solutions to their unspoken dreams.

So what about that other 35% – the reason people buy the products or services you offer, the actual product or service itself.

The product or service, and what that product or service does for your customer needs to be based not on what you "know" they ought to have, but on what you "know they know" they want.

If you are trying to sell your customers and prospects products and services because you 'already know' a solution you're still missing the mark.

Remember, the odds are good that your customers and prospects can buy very similar products or services from any one of several of your competitors.

Your advantage therefore needs to come from another source

– from your customers themselves.

Your starting point is to actually ASK your customers and prospects what they need solved, why it's so important to them, and what is the impact that having it solved will make on their business and their lives.

Only when you have the answers from their hearts and minds do you have the information on what you actually need to solve for them. That is when your product or service design begins.

USING BREAKTHROUGH POWER QUESTIONS

What has been your greatest fear or frustration?

What is the most critical number 1 thing you most want or need solved?

If you could have it any way you could imagine, how would it look?

What would change as a result of that?

Why is that important?

And why is THAT important to you?

A hidden benefit of taking the time to interview your clients and prospects about what they want solved is that they will give you the very language to use in telling them what you've designed for them. Their dreams, their challenges, their frustrations, and their goals. Their previously unspoken fantasy of what they wished their world looked like.

Here's another way to think about it. Remember Goldilocks and the Three Bears as she sampled their beds and bowls of porridge? She knew "just right" when she experienced it.

What experience is "just right" in your customer's mind?

Think of the word, "Professional." What image comes to your mind? Do you visualize a doctor, a dentist, a lawyer, or perhaps the president of a large corporation? Did the image of the owner or manager of the business you operate cross your mind? What criteria do you use to define a "professional?"

What about other people – your customers, for example? How do you think they define the style, personality, and results they're looking for?

The services you perform for your customers on a daily basis, such as progress check-ins, can have a big impact on them, their family, their staff, employees or customers if they have businesses, and their financial futures. The way you run your business and handle your customers' needs on a daily basis says a lot about you and the position you occupy in their minds.

BREAKTHROUGH PRINCIPLE 2

INSIGHT SHOWS UP...
WHEN YOU LET GO OF HOW YOU DO IT NOW

How do your customers see you? I mean, when the people you deal with on a regular basis, your customers and prospects – when they view you as the person they do, or are considering doing business with, who do they see?

Are you someone they might classify as a "typical salesperson" – someone who is out to sell them another product or service, or who is interested more in the sale or commission they'll earn?

Or do your customers and prospects view you more as a counselor – someone they like and can relate to and who is genuinely interested in them, and making sure they have the right product for their individual and specific needs, at the best possible price?

In the event that what they've purchased does not or will not work for them, or if you're not satisfied for any reason, what will you do to make things right? How you answer this basic and important question is critical to your success in business. It can mean the difference between enormous success, mediocrity, or even dismal failure.

Your Profitability Is Directly Tied To Your Establishing A Breakthrough Identity In The Minds Of Your Customers

And, it's a self-reinforcing mechanism, as well. If you are viewed by your customers as a time waster or a product hustler, even if it is not stated, you will tend to pick up that message yourself, and act accordingly, thus reinforcing your customer's image of you. On the other hand, if your customers welcome you as a counselor, or an advisor – someone with their best interests in mind – someone who can help them identify and solve their problems, they will feel good about you.

As a result, you will both feel good about yourself, and about the role you play for your customer.

You will be and act more professional, more confident, and will be better able to help your customer with the solving of his or her needs and problems.

As you fill the role as a problem solver, you can't help but reinforce and strengthen that positive image in both you, and your customer's minds.

So the first logical step is to learn and understand just what your customer's wants, needs and desires are.

And you find that out simply by interviewing and asking them. It is very important to listen carefully to what they say because sometimes there may be other, hidden or unstated wants or needs that may not be readily evident.

And only by fully understanding their needs, can you be of meaningful service to them.

So it is important to continually ask yourself (and be honest) the following question…

"How do your customers… the people who do business with you… your clients and prospects, see you?"

Here's an easy method you can use to find out.

Take a sheet of paper and draw a line down the middle.

On the left hand side at the top, label the column, "Products and Services."

Label the right hand column, "Help and Advice."

Every time you are in contact with a customer or prospect, whether they call you or you have a face-to-face meeting, evaluate the overall purpose of the meeting.

Did your customer or prospect look to you for the products or services you provide?

Or did they seek your help, advice or counsel to help them make a decision that would solve a particular need or challenge they were encountering?

Once you've determined that, place a mark in the appropriate column.

Next, ASK - Probe what it is specifically that they want solved. Find out whether that solution is actually best provided by a solution or approach they cannot find?

BREAKTHROUGH PROFIT MODEL TIP 3

Match Your Expertise to Their Need.

What product or service could you create to offer them and solve exactly that?

Then at the end of the month, evaluate the results of your list for two separate issues. If you have more marks in the "Products and Services" column than in the "Help and Advice" column, you pretty well know what perception your customers have of you.

Products & Services	Help & Advice

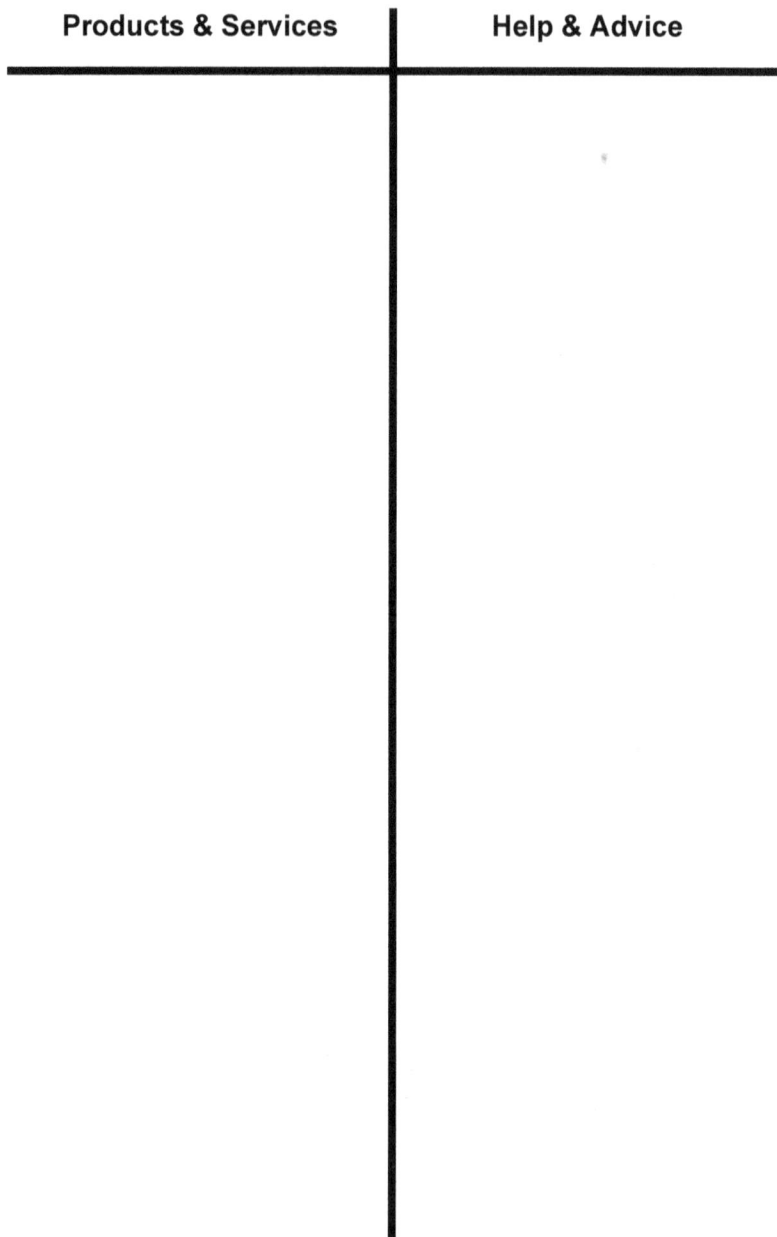

Equally important, you also know what you need to do to change that perception. You can then begin to develop and implement a plan of action that focuses on improving your image in the eyes of your customers.

"I can't change the direction of the wind, but I can adjust my sails to always reach my destination." ~Jimmy Dean

Once you've adjusted your sails, everything else is fine-tuning. Reliable studies demonstrate that the more needs a business handles for a customer, the longer they can expect that customer to do business with them.

Serve them, and test yourself again several months later. By comparing your evaluation sheets over the period of a year or two, you can easily see the Breakthrough progress you're making.

Identity is one-half of the formula.

The second half is fulfilling their dreams by solving exactly what they crave having solved.

BREAKTHROUGH PROFIT MODEL TIP 4

Create A Breakthrough Niche, Not A Copycat Offering.

Let's cut to the heart of the matter.

What you REALLY want is to eliminate the competition.

Here's how: what solutions did they name that you have the experience and expertise to fulfill?

And how many of them are looking for that very solution?

You've just unveiled a way to uniquely position yourself in their eyes, in the marketplace, and in a way your competition won't be able to challenge.

And to ensure you stay ahead of your potential competitors, make sure you stay in close conversation with your clients.

When you draw them into the solution design process they become more than clients - they become your PARTNERS.

Products?

Services?

Advice?

It matters not - they'll view you as their trusted advisor and you'll know what they want solved often before they've voiced it for themselves.

Even more powerful than having them as your Partners… is turning them into Advocates.

By definition, an "advocate" is someone who is a backer, a supporter, a promoter, a believer, an activist, a campaigner, a sponsor.

The last thing you need is a database full of one-product, or one-service customers who buy the minimum amount from you, complain about your prices every time they make a purchase, and give the rest of their business to the company or business who has the lowest prices or a "better deal."

There's no way you can make a profit on these types of customers. Besides, they make your life miserable and drive you crazy in the process.

Who you want are customers who not only give you all (or the majority) of their business, but re-buy from you repeatedly, year after year.

You want customers that are so happy and so pleased with what you do for them that they actively and enthusiastically campaign for you.

That the story they tell about you is so compelling, that the people they tell are nearly forced to call you and ask for your help.

Those are the people who make your job fun, enjoyable and profitable.

And PROFITABLE is the key word here...

If this is how you will be spending your weekday daylight hours (and for some of us passionate entrepreneurs, our evenings and weekends too), then it's critical to remember:

"The reason to be in business is to make a PROFIT!"

Profit is what gives you choices

Choices of who you want to work with

Choices of who you want to serve

Choices of who you want to play with

Choices of who you want to help grow and succeed

Choices of who you want to serve in your community

Those profits let you decide whether to grow the business, and how - what systems you want to put in place, what team members you want to have to delegate to, and programs and mentors you want to seek out to continue your own growth.

So while there are lots of details inherent in picking the strategy for your business, and the marketing you'll use, and how you'll deliver your products and services, there are two that you need to master right now to create a Breakthrough Business.

BREAKTHROUGH PROFIT MODEL TIP 5

Be The One Who Cuts Through Their Challenges.

Remember, they want to know WIIFM first. And then

BREAKTHROUGH PROFIT MODEL TIP 6

Make It Worth YOUR Time.

There are many choices you could make. You need to know WHY you're picking the profit model you select. Employee or Entrepreneur, the choices still hold.

For some folks, being an employee serves them best.

They know what is expected of them, how much they'll

earn, and when they have the rest of their time to themselves.

Other people, among them many of my clients, know that what will bring them joy and satisfaction when they get out of bed on a Tuesday morning is using their expertise and experience in an entrepreneurial challenge.

More time spent in designing and delivering and being in relationship with their customers AND much higher earning potential.

The trap that snags the unsuspecting is when they pursue their interests, or even use their internal story of "No one is going to tell me what to do…" yet their bank accounts are empty.

Let's get real! Money lets you create the life you want.

If we don't account for the money stress that eats at our minds and our health, then we're not accounting for the true costs and benefits of our chosen business model.

EVEN not-for-profits MUST make a "profit" each year to keep their doors open – it's called fund raising.

One of my colleagues and I were remarking on a local businessman. He'd been running a 'breakeven' business for 13 years.

What's a breakeven business?

He operated at a loss while his wife covered his expenses since he refused to get a job working for anyone and actually bringing in income.

I'll never get in the middle of a married couple's arrangements.

But ANY hourly income is better than that.

So first you need to know the value of the solutions you provide, and you need to charge that amount PLUS a profit.

Otherwise, why ARE you getting out of bed on Tuesday?

I propose that it's to use your time, attention, energy and inner brilliance, your gifts, to make a difference in the lives of others so that they reward you and you can create the life you want to live.

BREAKTHROUGH PROFIT MODEL TIP 7

Keep Your Customers For Life.

The Breakthrough idea is that by serving all the needs your prospects or customers have with the products and services you provide or have access to, you lock yourself in and the competition out.

And obviously, the longer you retain your customers, the more income you will earn from them, the more chances you will have to sell them additional products and services, and the more referrals you can get from them. It all adds up to increased profits for you.

Retention of your customers... the ones you've spent so much time, effort and money attracting and convincing to do business with you is critically important.

More than one study suggests that it costs six times more to get a prospect to buy from you than it does to get an existing customer to purchase from you again, and that it's sixteen times easier to sell an existing customer than it is a new prospect.

I've sure got better things to do with my money and my time than that!

When you add it all up, for every 5% increase in customer retention, you'll generate a 30% to 45% increase in profitability over an 18-month period.

Depending on the nature of the products and services you sell, if your repurchase rate isn't in the high 90 percentile range, you have some work to do. That's part of the focus of The Business Breakthrough System I use with my clients and program members, and the source of the keys I'm sharing with you here.

A lost customer is more than just a lost customer, and their attending profits.

It's much more. We'll be discussing how to determine what the actual cost of a lost customer is, and what to do to prevent them from leaving. But for now, just keep this important point in mind... if you're going to be successful in business, no matter what type of products or services you sell, you've got to have an intense focus on your customer.

Whether you choose to be an entrepreneur, a business owner, or an employee of a business, you've got to find out what **the customer** wants and do everything you can to help them get it.

And if you want to make a fortune rather than just a living, you can't do it for only a few.

BREAKTHROUGH PROFIT MODEL TIP 8

Get More Customers.

You must do it for large numbers of people.

Simply put… Build your customer base. Get more prospects to buy from you and become your customers.

You know how it works. When more people buy from you, you take in more gross dollars, and as a result (depending on your margins and overhead), you make more bottom line profits.

As a spin-off benefit, the more people you add to your customer base the larger it becomes. The larger your base becomes, the more people you have to go back to for additional sales and the referrals they're capable of giving you.

It's in this one single area where most business owners (including your competition, and probably, you, too, if you're honest), spend most of their time, effort and money.

If you've been in business for any length of time, you probably realize that getting new customers is not always the easiest, the most time-efficient, or most profitable thing you can do.

Most businesses only have one or two main methods of attracting new prospects to their businesses.

For example, you probably know that a large number of businesses are heavy in the use of telephone soliciting.

In fact, you, yourself, have probably gotten more than your

fair share of calls, when you were just sitting down for dinner.

Chiropractors, car dealers, truck driving schools, and personal injury lawyers take a different approach.

Many of them advertise heavily on television, especially during the afternoon hours to attract new customers.

They've found that a large part of their intended audience, the people who are most inclined to use their services, watch television during those hours, and it's a cost-effective way to reach them.

Each business, industry, or profession has their own methods and timing to contact those who are most likely to be interested in their products and services.

Some are offering their products and services on 'discount' time-limited offers through the Internet.

One dentist using Groupon's daily discount offering services got 400 new customers who never would have walked through his door.

The first-visit discount was recouped in the returning customers additional services at full fee, and their friends who came as well.

What works for some businesses, may or may not work for other businesses in the same or different industries or professions.

Including yours.

One of my consulting clients has a program for auditing compliance of complex insurance systems. That same system is as relevant in other industries she is expanding into. And each of those industries must be marketed to in different ways. In one industry it's by being known by the Chief Executive Officers, in another it's by being known by the Chief Financial Officers, and in yet another it's by being seen giving presentations to the Military Generals.

Think about your business and your company for a minute.

Chances are, that you, like nearly every other business owner in your industry or profession also utilizes one, or perhaps two main methods of attracting new prospects.

Most likely, the method you use is the same method that nearly every other business uses. It's called the, *"That's how things are done in our industry or profession,"* method.

Typically, when a person first chooses to go into business they look around and see what everyone else is doing.

Then they layout their office, shop or place of business just like every other similar type of business they've seen.

They look at what everyone else is doing to market or promote their businesses, products and services, and adopt those same marketing plans and methods to market or promote their business.

This activity isn't isolated to just a few businesses – nearly every business in nearly every industry or profession is guilty. But, wait a minute.

Who set up that system in the first place?

And who says it's right, or that it's the best system for you to use?

Do you get out and about on the weekends, where other

people gather?

If so, you may have noticed that the past four largest fast food successes were businesses who completely redesigned their food service presentation, ordering and delivery lines, and even self-service area presentations. I've seen it in ice cream shops, Southwestern snazzy health food restaurants, and so on.

The fact is, that there is an unlimited number of methods of attracting new customers to your business, and your imagination is the only limiting factor.

Some of the best, most productive and cost-effective methods you can use, can be adapted from what others are doing in totally unrelated businesses.

BE A PERPETUAL RESEARCHER

How observant are you?

What are others who are in the same business that you're in doing?

And, how effective are they?

Look around at what other businesses, unrelated businesses in other, unrelated fields, industries or professions are doing.

Have you seen what's working for them?

Is there one business that just stands out, by doing something different or unusual? Or, do they all pretty much use the same marketing methods? Next question: How creative are you?

Can you look at what some of the other businesses are doing, and adapt (with a few minor changes), their methods to your business?

In other words, if you were brand new, just starting in business, and had no idea of what anyone before you had done to attract new customers, what would you do?

How would you go about getting new customers? Would you use the same methods you use now, or would you do something completely different?

Want in on a secret?

Most of my clients and students confess they only read material directly related to their business and industry...

SO THEY ONLY THINK OF COPY CAT IDEAS!

I want you to break the mold - and to do that you need to be as clever as an Einstein ...

And that means subscribing to, and regularly reading, material that has nothing to do with YOUR specific business. The best sources I've found include "Entrepreneur" magazine and INC magazine. That's where people breaking the mold share their secrets.

A dentist I visited with specializes in working with children. He loves children. And he recognizes that as they get older, they may need braces, they'll probably get married, and have a spouse and children that will all need dental care. So, he set up his reception room with a special, kid-height counter, so when the children come in, they can talk directly to the receptionist, transact their business just as an adult would, and schedule their next appointment.

He's even decorated his reception area with artwork and pictures that some of his young patients have created. How do you think those young people feel? Well, you probably guessed it. They absolutely love it there. And they tell their friends about it, too. And their parents? They're *thrilled*.

Imagine, having your kids *want* to go to the dentist! And then be treated, not like a second-class citizen, but as an equal, transacting business (with the parent's help, of course), and having a hand in scheduling their future appointments.

What a learning and growing experience for them. And who do you think the parents use for their own dentist? That's right.

The spin-off business of catering to, and working with children, is their parents. First, whose hands will they prefer to have poking about in their own mouths?

Then, as the kids grow up and have families of their own, which dentist do you think they'll use, that they'll insist their spouse switches to, and that they'll bring their own children to? All as a result of thinking about relationship building as a System and putting each of the pieces in place in the business.

CREATE UNIQUE RELATIONSHIPS

The relationship this dentist is building with those young people, of friendship, of trust and of caring, will provide him all the financial security he'll ever need, and allow him to do whatever he wants, and go wherever he pleases for the rest of his life.

So, what about you and your business? What are you doing?

Specifically, what marketing system are you using, *right now* to attract new customers, and to build lasting relationships with them so they'll do business with you for a lifetime?

And second, how many *different* marketing methods do you

presently, and concurrently, have working for you? There's a real danger in having just one or two main methods of attracting new customers.

One of my consulting clients depended almost entirely on a telemarketing team to acquire leads for their clients' salespeople to follow up with.

When a well-funded competitor opened for business not far away, they hired nearly all that business' telemarketing staff, and nearly shut the business down. The business was nearly a total disaster.

When they called me in as a consultant, I could see that we had to do something quick, just to save the business. So, we got to work and hired and trained a whole new telemarketing crew, and got the business up and running again.

But that was just a quick fix. Here's the Breakthrough:

We needed a long-term system in place. So then we looked at other marketing options and put together an effective direct-mail program, started a proactive referral-generating system, and worked out some joint ventures and host-beneficiary relationships with other, complementary, but non-competing businesses.

Now, if something happens to any one of their marketing clients, they have other strategies or other elements of their Profit Model in place that can keep the business from collapsing, and keep it running smoothly.

What about your business? How can you apply this?

KEEP YOURSELF FRESH WITH NEW CUSTOMERS

Well, why not start by going back and revisiting the questions I asked earlier. Then see if there are some areas that you need to improve in. Make sure you're not dependent on only one or two main methods of attracting new customers.

New customers are important to your business, there's no question. But they're not just important. They're absolutely vital, not only to the growth of your business, but to the very survival of the business. It's critical that you have multiple systems in place to ensure that your business continues running, *and growing*, uninterrupted, if anything unexpected happens.

Because of the limited amount of space in these pages, we can't talk about all the methods of getting new customers, but in the training materials and workshops we conduct, we go into great detail on effective ways to attract prospects by the bushel, and convert them into loyal, long-term customers.

As important as getting more new customers is, there are still three more System elements you can use to grow your business.

And each of these activities is more profitable, more effective, and give you greater potential for leverage than the first one. Here's the next one:

BREAKTHROUGH PROFIT MODEL TIP 9

Get Your Customers To Make Larger Average Purchases.

In other words, increase the average transactional value of

their purchases. Or more simply, get them to spend more money when they buy something from you.

This just happens to be the quickest and easiest way there is to increase your profits. One of the things that continually amazes me is the number of businesses that have *extensive* and *expensive* plans in place to acquire more customers.

Yet, very few have paid much attention to this highly profitable, and high leverage step of increasing the size of the order getting more money from each of your customers every time they buy from you.

If you think for a minute about how easy this is and how profitable it can be, you'll see why it's such a powerful concept. And, you'll also see why nearly every fast-food restaurant has embraced, has mastered, and requires that every person who takes orders, understands, and is proficient in the use of the Up-sell and Cross-selling principles.

Think back about your own fast-food restaurant experience.

You drive up to the speaker and place your order, a sandwich and a drink.

And then what happens?

A voice comes back over the speaker and asks if you'd like an apple pie, or fries with your order.

That's an example of cross-selling. Selling an additional product in addition to, or beyond the initial purchase.

They might suggest that you 'Super-size' or 'Giant-size' your order, or add complementary products or services.

That's an example of an up-sell, increasing the size of the

initial order.

In any case, if you take them up on their suggestion, what they've done is just increase their profits *substantially*, since they made an additional sale, but had no acquisition or marketing costs.

How many *different* marketing methods do you presently, and concurrently, have working for you?

You see, they realize that a certain percentage of their customers will say, "Yes" And the only reason they say, "Yes" is because a suggestion was made to them. So they play the numbers game.

And the result?

Well, by being aware of what their customers might want, but not ask for on their own, and then by asking questions or making suggestions, they bring in a substantial number of dollars. And other than the actual cost of the product, those dollars are pure profit.

BORROW OTHERS SUCCESSFUL MODELS

Here's another technique fast food restaurants frequently use. It's called "Bundling," or "Packaging."

It's where they combine a sandwich, a drink and fries, then throw in a couple of "Bonus" items, like maybe a cookie and a toy. They put it all together in one package, and give it a name like "Happy Meal."

They'll charge you less for that package than what each of those items purchased separately would have cost, but the total dollar amount you spend will be higher.

And, since there were no marketing costs involved, other than the cost of the items, themselves, it's pure profit, and it goes straight to their bottom line.

Now, what does that have to do with you, and your business? Well, you may not be in the fast food business, but the same principles can still apply. Just ask yourself this question: "What other products or services do I have that would be natural complements to what my customers initially buy from me?"

Well, you know the answer to that and I won't go into all the details here. But for instance, if you have the type of business that offers more than one product to your customers you have a tremendous advantage to capitalize on the up-selling, cross-selling and bundling techniques.

Some types of businesses, such as insurance companies that may offer only one product or service can also benefit from these strategies by packaging certain policies that cover multiple family members, adding riders, or including other complementary services that go beyond the actual policies themselves.

Do these things seem like common sense to you?

Well, they probably do. But as I mentioned before, it's surprising how few businesses make effective use of these three simple principles.

Think about it.

In reality, you have an obligation to your customers, the people who trust you to provide them good quality products and services, give them sound advice and who hand over their hard-earned money to you, to make sure they get the very best value, the best use and the most enjoyment from their original purchase.

And if you have additional items, either products or services, that can enhance their value, their use or their enjoyment, then your obligation is to do everything that's reasonable and ethical to see that they at least have the option of taking advantage of those items.

Again, it's playing the numbers game. Some will take advantage of your offer, and some won't.

But at least you will have given them the opportunity, and you will have fulfilled your obligation to them.

You haven't made the decision for them. You've given them a choice, and you've let them decide.

If you come across as sincere, they'll not see you as being pushy, but they'll realize that you are really trying to do them a favor, to help them get more value, more use, and more benefit from their decision and their purchase.

If you've listened to what they want, their emotional ideas, words and signals, you'll be on target as you help them.

And they'll come back to do business with you again, and again, and will refer others to you, as well.

SELECT FROM PROFIT BOOSTING OPTIONS

Up-selling, cross-selling and bundling, these are only three of more than a dozen immediate, profit-producing methods you can use to skyrocket your business to the next level.

If you do nothing more than find a way to incorporate these three techniques in your business (which you should be able to do within the next twenty-four hours), you'll blast your profits completely through the roof.

Think about it: increasing your sales, increasing your *profits*, without increasing your expenses.

It's an exciting concept, and it can add an *immediate* twenty, thirty, even forty percent or more, *in pure profits* to your bottom line!

Now, let's move on to the next way to grow your business:

BREAKTHROUGH PROFIT MODEL TIP 10

Get Your Customers To Buy From You More Often.

In other words, increase the frequency of their purchases.

Get them to come back, Give them reasons to *want* to come back and to continue doing business with you.

The longer your customers go between purchases from you, the more chance they have of buying from your competition.

It's like, "Out of sight, out of mind."

You need to constantly stay in front of your customers with educational information, and notices of changes in the law or updates regarding the products or services they've purchased from you that can affect them.

And you need to tell them about new products, new lines, special incentives and other offers that might benefit them.

The idea, is two-fold: One, to "Lock" your customers in, so they can't afford to do business with anyone else, and secondly, to make it so attractive to do business with you, that they wouldn't even consider going anywhere else.

What you really want to do, is lead your customers to the inescapable and undeniable conclusion, that they would have to be completely out of their minds even to consider doing business with anyone else but you, regardless of the selection of products or services you provide, the prices you charge, your location, or the relationship they may have with the business they're currently doing business with.

Let me give you some real life examples of how this works: One of the clients I consult with owns a restaurant.

And for his business customers who like to take their clients to lunch, he offers a certain number of lunches for a pre-paid, discounted price. By doing this, he "Locks in" his customer, gets his money upfront, and makes it convenient for everyone.

The customer simply signs the check, which includes the tip.

No money changes hands during or after the lunch, and new customers are constantly being introduced to his restaurant.

As a result, many of those new customers take advantage of the same arrangement for their clients.

Here's another example.

The car wash where I take my cars offers a special pre-paid, discounted card, that's good for a certain number of car washes.

It's a great deal for me because I save money, and I can take my car to be washed.

And when my card is filled, I get a free wax job coming. It's a good deal for the car wash too, because they've gotten their money up front, and have locked me out of the competition.

Here's one more.

The store my client Tamara buys shoes from offers a "Points" program.

Every so often, she receives a notice in the mail informing her of how many points she's accumulated.

Now, she may not have been to that store for quite a while, but when she gets that notice and sees the credit she has coming, she nearly always makes it back to that store within just a couple days. And she hardly ever leaves empty handed.

Wait! Let's look at the whole new world of online and internet-based information marketing. This is the world in which you take your experience and expertise and turn it into information and trainings that others buy from you to learn and become more skillful and capable in their own right.

In this world, an entrepreneur can take their "know how" and create streams of products and programs, each one building on the one before, that have their customers coming back time and again for the next book, the next CD, the next 6-week course, the next special webinar for members only, and so on.

Think of everyone you do business with, day in and day out, for every day of your business and casual life.

How many different ways are you seeing people take their expertise and their know how and their experience and turn it into components of their profits model?

I'd like you to spend a week writing down all the examples you notice:

- ☐ Who really knows what their customers want?
- ☐ Who has created a Breakthrough Niche?
- ☐ What are the challenges waiting to be solved?
- ☐ What's the value in solving the challenges?
- ☐ What would tie customers to them for life?
- ☐ Who figured out how to get more customers?
- ☐ Whose customers increase their purchases or frequency of buying from them?

CASE STUDIES

My client **Jack** was recognized throughout his industry as the 'go-to' guy for creating the guidelines and the industry standards, working with the customers of those services, and then consulting to the mega corporations that needed to perform work to those standards for their clients.

For a decade, he'd been the key expert witness sorting out disputes when they reached the courts.

You might say he was the superhero expert.

The legal community across America became a user of his services when it came down to the final stages of disputes.

But that meant his personal income depended on things getting to the critical stage of the American legal system.

And who knew how often that would be?

The Breakthrough came in leveraging his expert identity but making it available in many tiers. We defined a service the legal community would value BEFORE their clients ended up in court and one no one else could easily duplicate.

Jack lived his life staying instantly conversant on every court decision that affected his industry, and he loved to write. Presto!

The average attorney has no spare time to keep up-to-date on court rulings that could profoundly affect their clients, to help them stave off problems ahead of time.

A new service to attorneys was born.

Sign up for an annual subscription to receive an instant electronic briefing within 24-hours of any ruling coming out of the courts, with Jack's insights on what that ruling could mean to your clients.

Or pay a lesser amount to receive an end-of-month summary newsletter.

Either option meant you get Jack's insights for the top gun in your industry so in turn you can provide stellar service to your own clients.

And you can still buy his hours for individual consulting.

For **Jack**, this was a Breakthrough on several levels.

He broadened his identity in the market place and solidified himself as the 'only' expert to listen to.

His subscription service leveraged his time, allowing him to serve many in the time he would have spent serving one AND getting paid multiple times for his effort.

His newsletter got him invited onto the speaking circuit in

front of the very folks he wanted as his individual clients.

Jack's Profit Model Breakthrough? Seeing his one-on-one clients could be drawn from hundreds of targeted subscribers.

Same expertise, same use of time he would spend keeping current on legal rulings, same information and insights, leveraged and made available at many price points, to a wider buying audience, completely smoothing out his income streams increases customer loyalty and multiple streams of profit.

Elaine, the jewelry design, needed a different business model redesign. She spread out 30 trays of her pieces all jumbled together and haphazard and said "Help!"

With her Vision and Goals set, we looked at her business model. We identified a Niche for her that would be high end unique and relatively high priced.

First we had to match her Vision to the ones her clients likely had. We reorganized all her jumbled and confused trays, reordering by type of stone, and style of the pieces themselves.

Instantly her products could be shown to boutique owners and private clients alike so that they could rapidly identify styles they wanted, and entire sets, collections and lines. The result was the size of her sales orders increased immediately. And fashionistas and TV stars are now wearing her jewelry in movies and on shows.

Seems simple, right? Obvious even?

Yet no other consultant she had met with noticed it.

Her best friend was an experienced independent sales rep who was ready and excited to take on selling for her.

Together they identified high-end boutiques in Los Angeles, San Francisco, Seattle, Vancouver, Hawaii and ski resorts where her key customers lived and vacationed. Beyond trunk shows. *Presto* - a Breakthrough Profit Model.

Nick's business was already producing 17 percent net profits in an industry with only three other competitors, each about his size.

His products were used across more than thirty industries and there was no compelling reason to narrow that list to a smaller niche to try to take on those competitors head to head for market share. Why?

When we surveyed everyone who had been in contact with Nick's company for the prior 24 months, either as a customer or just for information, we asked how they made their buying decisions for this equipment and the associated supplies.

Their answer was "last name seen is who we buy from" 80 percent of the time.

Not price. Not functionality. Last name seen on a flyer.

When someone on the manufacturing floor told procurement they needed that equipment or supplies, they reached in their inbox or drawer where they'd last tossed a brochure.

Knowing that information enabled us to reset the goals for our work. Rather than constructing complicated compensation models for regional distributors, time and resources were invested in identifying how to be the most present name in front of prospective buyers - marketing. Possibly through the distributors, possibly through other means.

Additionally, we focused on building auto-ship programs for

the associated supplies used in the function of the equipment, the highest margin part of the business. No name recognition required, just look at the container you just used - A Breakthrough in his marketing, fulfillment, and profits.

BACK TO YOU

We've been talking about your Breakthrough Profit Model here.

Airlines offer upgrades and mileage bonuses for those who fly with them on a regular basis. And countless other businesses offer similar programs as well.

They wouldn't sustain any of them if the math didn't prove that there was a positive Return On Investment - yes, PROFIT - that resulted from using each of their selected approaches.

Now, let's apply this concept to you and your business. What can you think of that you could do, that will endear your customers to you?

To lock them in, and get them coming back more often, and even refer others to do business with you?

Do you have an educational newsletter or special informative reports that you periodically send them, that keeps them updated? Do you send postcards, or do you have a website that keeps them informed of new items and promotions?

Do you hold special "Customer Appreciation Sales" or events? How about a frequent buyer club for your more loyal customers?

What about a Referral Reward system that recognizes or

compensates your customers for referring their friends?

You've got to let your customers know that you value them, that you appreciate them, that you want them to come back, and you want to make doing business with you fun, risk-free, rewarding, and easy.

Well, I'm sure you can see that the ideas are unlimited.

And while the restaurant, car wash and shoe store examples may not apply directly to your business, I've included them to serve as a stimulus so you can begin thinking of what you might consider applying in your business that can help you develop trust and loyalty with your customers.

In my coaching programs we go into great detail, and discuss more than two-dozen very specific strategies that create an almost magnetic effect, that keeps your customers returning time and time again.

We lead you by the hand and help you develop personalized and effective strategies that keep them saying, "I'll be back" strategies that keep them "Insulated" from, and locked out of your competition.

In the meantime, pull your team together and take them through this entire chapter with a flip chart, lots of pens and tape to put up new ideas on the walls.

Turn it into a brainstorming exercise with a prize for the best new ideas, or a piece of the profits for coming up with and implementing one that anchors your customers to you.

It's critical that you involve others on your team, as you'll see why when we discuss your Breakthrough Systems and Breakthrough Teams.

Let's get going on this Building Block today!

My Ah Ha's 💡

- ☐
- ☐
- ☐
- ☐
- ☐
- ☐

And now for your Action Plan.

BREAKTHROUGH ACTION PLAN

- ☐ Identify at least 2 sources you'll use to get fresh ideas that accomplish your Goals

- ☐ List each of the ways you do your marketing today to build relationships

- ☐ Expand the list to include at least six different approaches you could use - products, programs, services, etc.

- ☐ Decide what solutions you want to create and the greatest opportunity you could seize

- ☐ Create a pricing list of the transaction values you offer

- ☐ Organize how you'll make "Up-sell" and "Cross-selling" offers

- ☐ Design bundles or packages to offer

- ☐ Design "Bonuses" you can deliver to stay in front of your Customers and make new offers

- ☐ Calendar how and when you do each of these, including systematizing them

- ☐ Review the tools, resources, information you need, and organize them

See www.BreakthroughByDesign.com/gold

FIVE
FIVE
FIVE

ANTI-PRICING

What comes to mind when someone tells you the price of their service or product? Do you throw up your defenses? Instantly start mentally tearing the value down? Emotionally start critiquing everything about them? Rationalize why they must know what the 'right' price is?

Welcome to the human race and our wiring when it comes to the value of 'money.' Price is important, don't get me wrong. It's very important. And it carries a lot of weight in a prospect's buying decision. The same chatter is running in their minds.

But it's only one of many factors that a person considers when making their buying decision, if you get the sequence right. People buy emotionally, then justify their decision.

Here's what I mean.

In actuality, there's very little difference in insurance policies issued by any number of insurance companies in the same geographical area.

General overhead costs, utilities, phones, supplies, wages, and product costs are also similar for most companies that sell like products and services.

And likewise, there's usually very little difference in the products or services you sell versus those same types of products or services sold by your competitors.

So, if all those factors... similarity of products and services, overhead costs and product costs... are pretty much the same, the prices charged by each individual business must, out of necessity, be pretty close, as well.

It's true, that one company may, for example, obtain a lower purchase price on their products and as a result, be able to offer a more attractive sales price for a certain period of time.

But eventually, things change and the playing field becomes pretty level once again.

Meanwhile, businesses that become fixated on price competitions often price themselves into unprofitable offerings and destroy their business altogether.

There are other factors not to be overlooked such as investment income and tax write-offs or advantages that can play a role in the prices businesses charge for the things they sell.

But overall, all things considered, the prices charged for the goods and services from one company to another similar company are going to be fairly close over the long haul.

As soon as you develop a new product, or offer a new service, it's just a matter of time before your competition latches on to it and offers the exact same thing, or maybe enhances it and offers it for a lower price.

Copycat moves take place in the automotive industry, in the clothing industry, in banking services, in insurance products. We've seen it in manufacturing processes, in legal specializations and on and on.

The point is, that... no matter what business you're in... As soon as you lower your prices, your competition can do the same thing. Everyone gets to play with this Building Block.

BREAKTHROUGH ANTI-PRICING TIP 1

You will never maintain, long-term, a competitive advantage because of the products you offer, or the prices you charge.

Please, don't tell me "But Linda, I run a yoga studio. It's different for me."

I promise you, as soon as you try to use pricing to draw clientele you'll lose your pricing-based customers when the studio down the street runs a promotion.

The marketplace you operate in is so fiercely competitive...

so cutthroat… so unforgiving… that you absolutely must do something to differentiate yourself from your competition.

If you don't, you'll be relegated to just another "me-too" business, just like all your competitors.

Now… you want to know the good news?

That's how your competitors operate… in a "ME-TOO!" mode.

Just look around. They're all the same.

Their businesses all look the same.

Their products are all the same.

They walk and talk the same.

And their advertising all looks like and says the same things as the next guy's.

BREAKTHROUGH ANTI-PRICING TIP 2

Your competitors' lack of understanding how to change gives you a tremendous Breakthrough opportunity!

You see, if they keep on doing what they've always done… they'll keep on getting what they've always got. But you… if you want to get something different… you've got to be willing to make some changes.

And that's what this is all about. Build the emotional

"value" of the solutions you're giving them first, and price won't matter. Saves Time. Makes It Easier. Expands My Reach.

CASE STUDIES

Remember my client **Susan** and her marketing strategies business? Guess what shifting meant for her business?

In addition to repositioning her team members attention on both the language they used with clients, and on the language they used while delivering results to the customer, Susan *raised* her fees 20 percent above the rest of the market. Clients continued to sign up – they saw the value and were happy to pay for it.

And as a bonus – two of her problem customers used the increase in fees as their reason to go away, and her entire team breathed a sigh of relief at being able to spend their days working with customers who appreciated them!

It's not always about bundling services or products into a fixed price to simplify things.

My client **Jacob** provided services that could be viewed as a commodity. When he let his conversations with prospects focus on the prices he charged, he closed 30% of the prospects.

Then he got a call that he handled differently.

Rather than let them ask their typical "How much would it cost?" question, he asked them "How much is at risk economically in this matter?"

They named a range in the millions of dollars. He then responded, "Then you need to let us do our job and find the best result available for you." With the value of the issue on the table, they said "Yes!" and he had a Breakthrough in Anti-Pricing.

Nick's customers loved his doing their usage tracking and offering just-in-time auto-ship. They were happy to pay a reasonable rate to not have to manage that in-house.

BACK TO YOU

Remember our discussion about getting out and interviewing your current customers and prospective customers? Go back and look at what you were told and identify how you can take an "Anti-Pricing" approach in your business.

BREAKTHROUGH ACTION PLAN

☐ Go back through your list of what prospective clients want to have solved

☐ Estimate the economic value your results can create for their business and life

☐ Expand the list to include at least six different approaches you could use in pricing

☐ Create a pricing list by the values you offer

☐ Design 3 bundles or packages to offer and use them with your very next prospective customer, or new offer to current customer

See www.BreakthroughByDesign.com/gold

SIX
SIX
SIX

SYSTEMS

Sometimes even the best-laid plans can unexpectedly blow up in your face and birth a crisis.

People make mistakes, technology breaks down, "drama" happens. The phone rings and a customer is yelling. We've all been there when the panic sets in and all rational thinking hits the road. My client **Elliot** learned that when he say and stated at the two reports on his desk – client complaints on the firs, and client turnover on the second.

When Elliot started his company he imagined he'd build his business and it would grow from success to success. Now he was faced with a stalled business and a looming sense of overwhelm.

He couldn't grow it fast enough to keep up with the clients who were canceling their orders or not renewing. This wasn't matching how he thought it would go when he launched his business.

While the key to handling a crisis or what we sometimes refer to as a fire, is to become a highly skilled Fire Fighter, the goal for your business, or Elliot's, should be to minimize the number of fires you have to put out... so you can spend your time and attention on high payoff activities. Activities that will produce critical, profitable results.

Elliot had the choice of thinking he needed to increases sales to 'solve' the situation, or to breakthrough to notice what actually needed fixing.

BREAKTHROUGH PRINCIPLE 3

RESULTS ARE EASY...
WHEN YOU DESIGN EVERY ACTIVITY
TO ACHIEVE THEM

What Elliot needed was to design and install "Systems."

Why? Because your time is precious and one of your key goals needs to be running your business in a fashion that minimizes duplication of efforts, that limits the amount of time that is wasted, and the result of your work has your clients adoring you and wanting everything you offer them.

That means that not only your time, intelligence, attention and energy but that of every single person you invest in as an employee or vendor needs to be well-designed.

The most acclaimed and successful businesses are those that invest the time and brainpower to sort out how to 'simplify', 'streamline', 'optimize' and 'ease' all of the activities of their business - the daily Building Blocks of their operation.

BREAKTHROUGH SYSTEMS TIP 1

Everything you DO in your business is a system.

The focused assessment I conducted showed Elliot that he was missing multiple "systems" that ensure a business keeps running, *and growing*, both day in and day out and even when the unexpected happens. You need these systems in place too.

More systems in place mean each person is freed up to use their highest skills and thinking for delivering the best customer results, using the teamwork, customer service, and problem solving of high performers.

How to create that result? By putting practical processes, procedures, policies and standards for doing things in place, they get predictable, reliable high payoff returns on everyone's efforts. There is a series of steps to take, in each aspect of your business to design, test, and deploy systems.

But before we dive into the specifics I want you to consider several core areas that need your attention 'soonest'– the same systems that Elliot was missing. Each one supports your success, whether you are a solo entrepreneur or a leader of a growing business:

- ☐ Customer Facing Systems
- ☐ Administrative Systems
- ☐ Management Systems

Each of those areas has activities, executed by the members of your team, in interaction with each other and with your vendors and customers. Even when 'computerized' and automated, those activities are systems.

Elliot and I laid out a concise action plan for getting key systems in place. As he designed and installed each one, it freed up more time and attention to focus on critical activities like building joint venture relationships, designing new products for his ideal customers, and spending time on what mattered most – his family.

Let's start with the source of your revenue, your customers.

CUSTOMER FACING SYSTEMS

Elliot and I talked about the five *principal* ways to grow a business – any business:

- ☐ Increase your customer base
- ☐ Deliver excellent customer service
- ☐ Increase your customer retention
- ☐ Get your customers to make larger average purchases
- ☐ Get your customers to buy from you more often

The truth is that other than some administrative functions, some of which are not under your direct influence or control, nearly everything you do to build or grow your business can be classified under one of those four different and distinct areas, or categories. If you learn this one simple concept and how to apply it, believe me, your competition won't stand a chance.

But here's where business after business collapses into disaster - they think it's all about the work… and only about the service or product work they do for their clients.

So let me ask you - have you EVER called in on the direct line to your business, as if you were your own customer? I mean, have you called in and heard what your customer hears rather than dialing in to your voicemail box.

I stood at my client **Mark's** counter and listened to his receptionist say "Hi, Jen here." That was the total greeting at the inbound phone line of a multi-million dollar company. Do I really need to point out that's not the way to brand your business day in and day out?

Any business that wants to be seen as 'professional' would be wise to create standard procedures for Telephone Skills and Etiquette, and check how they're being used 2 or 3 times a year.

Your customers and prospects had better love the way they're treated at every encounter including when they call that line. WHY? Because your customers, just like Mark's will seldom tell you when they've had a lousy or offensive experience, they'll just hang up and go away.

And your prospects won't pass that "entrance gate" to your business, so you'll never know they were about to knock on the door and ask to speak to you.

THEY WON'T SAY GOOD-BYE

Last year, more than 200 million Americans stopped doing business with companies that they were 'Satisfied' with. And sixty percent of so-called "satisfied" customers switch companies or brands on a regular basis.

Here's an interesting point: Most business owners know exactly how much they have tied up in furniture, fixtures and equipment. They can tell you, nearly to the penny, how much each item costs, how old it is, how much it's depreciated and what the remaining life expectancy is.

That's important information for any business to have. There's no question about it.

But what's amazing is that very few business owners have any idea of what the value of their most important asset is - their customers. All too often business owners tell me "I don't have time or money to spend on figuring out that mundane stuff out." This was Elliot's first reaction too.

You're missing the point if that's your mindset: We're talking about each activity IN your business that attracts great customers, satisfies their needs, bills them and collects your revenue rapidly.

This IS your business. Each one of those areas needs your time and attention, periodically, regularly, deliberately to determine if you can refine the way you get things done - your way of working - your systems.

Deliberate attention with the goal of doing each and every activity reliably, repeatedly, with excellence, no matter WHO is doing it.

Think about how this concept relates to your entire business for a minute. I've included an extensive discussion about how to estimate the acquisition costs and revenue value to your business. You'll find it in **Appendix A**.

So right now grab a pen and paper.

Calculate the actual cost of acquiring and loosing a client. And the one time cost of putting a system in place to *keep* them.

The cost of acquiring a customer: _____

The cost of losing a customer: _____

The cost of installing a system: _____

Obviously it's time to talk about systematizing each activity that can affect your customer's experience of you, your team, your products and services.

YOUR SUCCESS DEPENDS ON THEIR EXPERIENCE

First of all, who are your customers - those who are buying from you now? Do you know why they purchased a certain type of product or service?

Do you know what their challenges, fear or hopes are? What about your staff or employees? Do you know how they treat or feel about your customers? Do they, or do you, for that matter, have *favorite* customers? What makes them a "Favorite?" Is it how much they spend? How often they come in? What is their personality?

And how do you treat those customers? Any differently from the others? How do you decide which customers you give the 'best' to?

Do you have regular staff meetings and talk about "how to think like a customer?" What would you want if you were a prospect considering doing business with you for the first time?

What would encourage an existing customer to give repeat business to your establishment or organization? Or to considering refer a friend, a family member or an acquaintance?

Do you have a training system in place to teach your staff how to handle or deal with difficult customers? Short-tempered customers? Analytical customers?

Do you have a plan for moving people up the "Loyalty Ladder?"

From Suspect to Prospect to Browser. Then on to Customer, Client, and Advocate. And finally to convert them into Raving Fans?

When a customer stops doing business with you, do you know why? Do you have a *system* in place to find out? Do you have a system for managing the timing and content of your marketing messages to your prospects and clients?

What would you have to do differently to get your customers to buy from you for, say, 6 years, instead of just 5 years?

Iif you will actually take the time to go through these questions and formulate answers for them, and then incorporate that information into your business practices, you can work wonders towards extending the buying lifetime of your customers. As a result, you'll add *significant* profits to your bottom line.

Elliot and I spent a lot of time considering things from his customer's point of view - after all that's where the revenue comes from. When Elliot formalized taking the time to go through these questions with his team, and incorporated their ideas into his business practices, he measurably extended the buying lifetime and profitability of his customers. As a result, he added *significant* profits to his bottom line.

I've provided a list of questions for you to use, on your own or with members of your team, to create Breakthroughs in your thinking and the design or your systems in **Appendix B.**

Now it's time to look at the second part of the equation - what does it 'cost' you to accomplish the rest of your business AND how can you increase the reliability of every activity while reducing the effort and expense.

Here's the next crucial category.

ADMINISTRATIVE SYSTEMS

Remember that idea of being prepared to be a fire fighter when things go wrong?

It took time for Elliot to understand that he goal of systems is to make things go right, easily, over and over again, no matter who is getting the work done. There isn't enough room in this chapter to outline every possible process in his business or yours, and that's not the point. The point is to create a Breakthrough in your thinking, including how you recruit, hire, train and pay team members, run meetings and make decisions, when and where supplies are ordered, vacations are requested and booked on the calendar, sales contracts reviewed, repair logs monitored, and so on.

Each of those activities is a system.

When and where are supplies ordered, vacations requested and booked on the calendar, sales contracts reviewed, repair logs monitored, and so on – systems.

When legal and regulatory issues are in play, it's best to buy the time of experts in human resources, accounting, inspection and compliance to ensure you've set those systems up in the best manner. For all other systems, the most powerful and useful systems are designed by the actual users themselves.

At your business start-up stage you can get that information from advisors and mentors and books and courses. As your company grows, all the refinements and redesigns that create Breakthrough results are best designed with the involvement of the users and participants in the activities themselves.

If you've never done this before, a coach or consultant can guide the process with you and your team to demonstrate the process and guide and give feedback as you master it for yourselves.

You need everyone to own and use the system. This can be created, and the systems trained, during group meetings where the Team discusses best practice and shares their own tips and techniques and designs the improvement plans.

Remember, each one of your staff members really does make a difference to your success - and it can be a profitable business IF their behavior is systematized. Managing that team is the third set of your systems:

MANAGEMENT SYSTEMS

OK - I need to share with you a conversation I keep having in businesses large and small throughout this country. I have this conversation nearly weekly.

Client: "How do I get these folks to make decisions, take action faster and do what they 'should' be working on?"

Linda: "When did you last discuss it?"

Client: "They should just know!"

Linda: "Why would they know what you want them to focus on?"

Client: "It's obvious what they should be doing"

Linda: "If you've never discussed it, why would it be obvious?"

Client: "Anyone with a brain …"

Linda: "Oh, so you run your business on mind reading? How's that been working for you?"

Client: "I don't have time to tell people everything!"

Linda: "First, if they've never in their life worked for a skillful manager, or been in a good meeting or seen it modeled, where would they have learned how to discuss what needs doing, make decisions and report back? In high school?"

Client: "OK, I get your point. How much time is this going to take to really make this work better?"

No matter their profession or the size of their business, they practically growl at me.

I have a saying I use in many of my talks. It goes something like this: "People say the biggest fears we have are of public speaking, death, and taxes. In fact there's a fourth fear and it's more important than all the others. People's Number One Fear is of Managing!"

For Elliot, and others, that fear was for a perfectly obvious reason. They never worked for a competent manager, so they've never seen or never learned how to organize their thoughts and information, share it with others, solicit their input, turn it into decisions and action plans, and move on.

Read that again. Really.

Read that paragraph over and over until you get it.

You're not to blame if you've felt reluctant to step into increasing competence as a Leader and Manager.

As a result of not experiencing great managers, most people running businesses don't know how to recruit, hire, delegate to, direct, give feedback, guide or problem solve. This is their personal "rock of Sisyphus."

That is the most important paragraph in this chapter, perhaps this book. Don't think for a moment that I said it casually.

I'm profoundly grateful for the accidental career path that gifted me with the opportunities I've had to work with smart, gifted, skilled business people I could model, learn from, be mentored by.

And I know how few people have had those experiences.

My passion is helping YOU become the most effective leader of your chosen business so that you can "pay it forward" by teaching those you work with the Breakthrough skills you learn and use.

For instance, I coach CEOs, presidents, VPs and managers, professionals and entrepreneurs - all the way through the organization - to get their system for holding effective meetings and discussions turned into their Way of Working.

Do nothing more than that and you'll create Breakthroughs in your business in 30-minutes flat on topics that have been languishing for weeks, or even months.

BREAKTHROUGH SYSTEMS TIP 2

One of the most important skills of a competent manager is running effective meetings.

I work with my clients and program members on the details of the topics they need to cover to get things running smoothly in their business. One of the most important and least known is "what type of meeting to hold."

Elliot complained to me "Nothing is accomplished but wasted time, repeating conversations month after month, and my teams walked out without the information they need." Everyone was perpetually aggravated. He was holding the wrong meetings at the wrong time on the wrong topics.

You'll find a guide for sorting out which type of meeting to hold in "**5 Meetings Defined"** which you'll find in **Appendix D** as a framework for your conversations and work together, and **Appendix E** outlines how to hold productive meetings..

I had Elliot list every topic where an issue had been languishing, waiting for a decision to be made for weeks or months. The right meetings let him pinpoint where the breakdown took place and get his team focused on solving it.

When you learn how to determine what you're trying to achieve or solve, identify and use the specific styles of meeting to create a Breakthrough for your stalled team.

Here's a critical Management System you need in place:

A system for making decisions!

In my programs and consulting work, I teach my **7-Steps for Solving Any Issue**.

At the heart of it is the fact that for over 20 years I've walked into organizations where everyone was pointing fingers at each other and declaring "they" were stalling, stonewalling, back-burnering, making stupid decisions, or just plain doing it wrong,

Each and EVERY time I dig through what is going on it's one of two things.

A - They're facing an unsolvable "Paradox"

B - They don't know how to solve solvable issues

Even with all the case studies provided in this book, you'll only learn to master each of these with practical experiences. Let me give you some examples.

Nick's VP of Sales, Mary, had made and agreement with a

new Regional sales representative who violated the rules set up for how to pay reps. Karen, the controller, refused to allow the agreement to go through and be set up for payment.

While their offices were 50-feet apart, they were so enraged with each other not seeing things their way that they created an email argument thread that went on for 11 pages.

He handed it to me and asked, "What am I supposed to do about this?"

He had hoped that the two of them would "sort it out," but they couldn't – each had a sound reason for what they were trying to do on behalf of the business.

BEWARE Of PARADOXES

A paradox shows up when two people are arguing from completely correct points of view, that just happen to conflict with each other. They can argue, point to policies, put together elaborate analyses and spreadsheets, and shout about what is 'right'… It makes no difference because no one in the discussion is actually wrong, so each is unlikely to budge or change perspectives.

The only system that solves a paradox is to elevate the issue up one level in the organization and have someone higher up make a policy decision about how that issue will be handled in the future, and notify everyone about the decision.

Period.

So the solution to Nick's Paradox was that it needed to be raised in a business-matter-of-fact discussion (a Breakthrough in and of itself) so that HE could make a business policy decision about how things would be handled, in this instance and in any others that might occur. No more email wars!

When you find yourself in head to head dispute, take a step back and ask yourself if you might be caught in a Paradox, and need to elevate the point of view on the matter.

Meanwhile, very few people know the reason things stall, or the wrong decisions are being made is because one of the steps got lost while they were trying to solve the situation.

What was missing in your systems the last time you needed to solve an issue, a challenge, a complaint?

STICK TO THE STEPS

After years of being asked to come in and settle disputes and calm the waters of teams that were dragging their heels rather than working together to solve things, I spotted the pattern.

People don't know HOW to systematically solve issues.

BREAKTHROUGH SYSTEMS TIP 3

Every issue can be solved if dealt with systematically.

There are seven identifiable steps for working through any issue, any problem, any innovation. Anything. On your own or in a group. The topic itself doesn't matter.

Each time I'd listened to the content of the disagreements team member laid out for my consideration, I could pinpoint which step had been skipped. As a result, I drew up a diagram and list of the steps and took it with me to my next client meeting.

When I showed it to the team, the light went on for everyone. I had them list every topic where a decision had been languishing, each decision that had been waiting to be made for weeks or months. Then I asked them to pinpoint where the breakdown took place. And every time they were able to identify it for themselves. A true Breakthrough for that team!

You'll find the "**7 Steps To Solve Any Issue**" guide which I teach all my clients in **Appendix F**. They work to solve issues in crafting the Building Blocks of your Customer Facing Systems, Administrative Systems and Management Systems alike.

CASE STUDIES

My client **Leonard** and his Sales managers watched the economy squeeze their industry. They knew that the upcoming management meetings were about the number of sales staff they should cut by the end of the month.

They worried constantly because they were also facing management pushing new products to the sales team that they didn't believe could be sold profitably.

Using my **7 Steps To Solve Any Issue** in two working sessions they built a compelling business case and got their Finance Department's agreement to hire two more sales managers, and to change the compensation model for the sales team to trigger even higher sales results.

Furthermore, they got Human Resources to allocate a further $20,000 for developing a new recruitment process to identify a high potential sales staff before they were hired and weeks of training investment was made on new hires.

Next, they used the same steps to create a case for a market test on the proposed new products to identify if there were a profitable price that would work in the market place, before retiring already profitable products.

A Breakthrough on multiple fronts for the team and the company!

Mastermind member **Roseanne** had a combination counseling and information products business. Her vision included taking each topic she was a recognized expert in, and turning them into both live programs and recorded products. Her goal was to grow a 6-figure business to high-6-figures in 18 months.

When we sat down and organized her ideas, she had seven different products and programs in mind. Moreover, she had a 'plan' to launch each of the seven products in a six-month span. And none of the material had yet been drafted.

Now you might think this it the point at which we burned the plan. Not quite. Instead we went back through the list. Together we figured out which could be written and recorded the fastest, and began to lay out the common detailed steps of every part of the launch. The criteria for success were specific sales volumes within 14 day of each launch.

We then prioritized which single launch would have 100% focus. Roseanne selected a product that related to an upcoming holiday challenge, with a six week target launch date. We pushed each next, more complex product, out on 90-day rollout schedules.

What became apparent was that there were no skills on board to accomplish the 376 tasks involved with the product creation and launch. So the next step was to locate the skills and systems in outsourced vendors, so that Roseanne could focus on content production.

Without the systems being put in place, none of the launches would have taken place at all, let alone on time. With them we added six figures to her business quickly.

Elaine, the jewelry designer, assumed she'd have to be the one doing it all. She was completely open to figuring out how to 'do it all' differently. We created Breakthroughs in several arenas. First we detailed exactly the talent she needed to train and trust handing off duplication of her pieces. Brainstorming revealed she'd be able to find them in workers at the shops where she bought her gems and supplies. We designed the system she used to time herself making a second version, to detail the steps she would use to train her staff and to evaluate how long it was taking them to replicate each one with the quality she wanted.

With those steps in place she knows each piece will be manufactured exactly how she wants, creating her **Breakthrough System**.

BACK TO YOU

While Leonard is managing a multi-million dollar sales operation, your business doesn't need to be that big before you use systems.

For instance, when I was earning nearly $200,000 a year doing private consulting and hosting my on-line radio show, I quickly knew I needed to set up a system.

Each week I spoke with upcoming guests, sent them written confirmation of the date of their appearance on the program, got the marketing materials together to advertise each episode, and so on. Three hours each week. And then on broadcast day there were 17 steps. I had to set up all the electronic gear for recording the program as backup for the on-line system, laying out the profile materials from the guest with my prepared questions, etc.

Without a system it was too easy to forget a step. Without a system I had to rely on memory for all of those activities, and memory can sure be faulty. I know – goofed a couple of times when I missed steps.

With a system, written and in a binder, I got everything accomplished in one-half the time, error-free, every week.

Whether you are doing it on your own, working with a consultant or coach, the path to getting systems in place starts when you schedule working sessions to get it done.

The most effective meetings will be those with the other people who contribute to the activity or participate in it, or even are the receivers of the results. Use the guides you'll find in Appendixes C and D as a framework for your conversations.

Keep asking everyone "How could this be done better?" which may mean 'faster' or 'easier' or 'with fewer touches' or in 'half the time' or 'with fewer mistakes and less waste' and so on.

Make a list of every suggestion, prioritize the ones that can make it easier, faster, more accurate, and so on and decide together how you'll use the **7 Steps For Solving Any Issue** to design and implement improvements to the process.

Once you have the process documented, turn the step-by-step lists into your Training Materials, and have another person do the task just following those steps. Any questions they have become the additions and adjustments to the procedures of your system.

Keep asking every year "How could this be done better?" Ask your staff, ask your customers, ask yourself!

Put it all on a Breakdowns List.

As for the complex systems behind making sure you're getting your taxes paid accurately and on time? Get your CPA, Controller, CFO to sit down for a working session to review your goals, and what you're doing in the business, and put documented systems in place. Let's make sure you don't get any surprise visits from the IRS!

The Breakthrough we want for you is to cut down on your effort, ensure your time is spent on activities that need your brain power, make as much profit as possible and keep as much in YOUR pocket as is possible and legal.

Now it's your turn. Go read each of the **Appendixes**. Take notes as you read them so that you can decide which elements you want to make a priority for yourself and your team.

You might decide to give them this book to read so they share your understanding of the matters and can participate as teams taking on individual issues to solve them and to design and install new systems.

Finally, systems let you measure.

WHAT GETS MEASURED GETS ATTENTION

When you install a system, document it and train everyone to use it, you create a baseline for performance that is the foundation for measuring

- [ ] whether team members understand and successfully use the system with the standards you set

- [ ] whether the results match what you wanted the system to create and your customer is looking for

- [ ] whether the activity is profitable in time, attention and energy used, including customer retention

- [ ] whether one activity is interfering with another rather than working together to grow your business

- [ ] whether the activities are getting your Goals accomplished

No matter how thoroughly you 'discuss' a topic with your team, no matter how many heads nod when you close a meeting by saying "So, we're agreed that Jerry will get that done by Tuesday at 3," no matter how much you believe you've removed obstacles from everyone's path, business days are loaded with demands, interruptions, distractions and shifting priorities.

When you put metrics in place, by Goal, by system, by activity, you create the decision-making criteria everyone needs in order to hold herself accountable for getting the most important, highest payoff activities done first.

Metrics can include cost of sales, return on investment to create and deliver your products, marketing, technology and so on. But that's not all.

One of the best articles I ever read (and have now shared with 1,000s of clients, students, readers, radio listeners and more) was published in Fast Company. It's called **Measure What Matters**, and it's the result of interviews with leaders in many different industries about the metrics they consider most vital to the success of their business. Everything from Customer Joy, to turnaround time, to ... well I won't use up your time up here on listing endless ideas.

I recommend you get yourself a copy of that article, give a copy to everyone on your team, and sit together to identity the sweet spot that you can measure that will make all the difference in the world to your customers and your results.

That's Breakthrough leverage!

My Ah Ha's

- ☐
- ☐
- ☐
- ☐

BREAKTHROUGH ACTION PLAN

☐ Identify 1 Customer-facing, 1 Administrative and 1 Management breakdown to improve

☐ Download the Article 'Measure What Matters' from the Fast Company archives and read it with your entire team.

☐ Develop your metrics list and the systems you need to set up for those activities

☐ Ask everyone who touches each activity to join in listing the steps you currently use in those processes or systems

☐ Ask "How could we do this better?"

☐ Use the guides in the Appendixes to determine what needs to be started, stopped and continued

☐ Organize how you'll make changes to the systems you use and who should participate

☐ Design how you'll train others to use the new system and monitor the results you're getting

See www.BreakthroughByDesign.com/gold

Systems ensure you make 'excellence' in serving your customers and running your business itself your "New Normal".

SEVEN SEVEN SEVEN

TEAMS

Imagine what it would feel like if you could get out of bed on Tuesdays with the confidence that you will be more effective at keeping YOUR attention on the High Payoff activities that need your attention, while you easily hand off the rest of what needs to get done to an outstanding team.

All of us in business have a dilemma we struggle with. It's the question "When is it time to hand my work off to someone else… and how will I be sure they'll be a high performer?"

Many of my program members say solving this one thing alone would make them a better, happier, and more productive business person. It's the key to rescue them from getting caught in the 'small' stuff that clogs up the flow of business activities.

"It's team work that makes your dream work!"

~ The Sherman Brothers

Teams are one of the most emotional elements of building and running a company, any company. Dealing with other people makes most of us fear we're incompetent. So in many ways we take the longest to solve these three issues than any others:

* How to know when to hand off work to other people?

* Who to hire and trust to get what needs to be done... and DONE WELL?

* How to find staff or outsource to 'experts and doers'

The mystery of it all is due to never experiencing the cycle of recruiting, hiring, training and managing for ourselves when we're employees inside organizations. Throughout our work life, it all usually takes place out of our line of sight.

And if we're entrepreneurs, we usually started as a technical expert who again never saw 'hiring' done well.

My clients and students usually opt to hire a friend of a friend, or the first 'good resume' or 'nice' person they interview. And then they spend months and years muttering about how dissatisfied they are, but that it's too much effort to get rid of her and get someone better. Sheesh!

It's time to see your team as a PROFIT Center rather

than an expense. Delegate and distribute everything that distracts you from the highest and best use of YOUR time, attention and energy!

Ironically it's not that hard to accomplish - several basic steps and taking the time to find the 'right' choice instead of the 'convenient' or available ones - and it's all learnable.

Each time you dash ahead and skip the steps you'll end up complaining and settling rather than raving about your team.

BREAKTHROUGH TEAM TIP 1

High Performance Teams require patience time, attention, commitment.

By now you may have heard about Zappos, the online shoe seller who hires people, makes everyone work on the phone order calls and in shipping and fulfillment first, and then offers them *thousands* of dollars to go away. All to check that each person hired appreciates the customer, the purpose of all her work, and is a true fit with the rest of the team. Now THAT is a Breakthrough Team Building system!

You don't have to be a 'billion dollar business' to value the team you're building highly enough to take the time and efforts to find 'perfect fits'. They're a critical Building Block for your success and business growth.

You can be my jewelry designer client Elaine, locating staff experienced in handling the tools and resources of her jewelry trade. Or be attorney Jack, needing to find the ideal associate to hand off repetitive document filings.

So let me share with you the keys to building your Breakthrough Team: Know When To Hire! It sounds mundane, I know, but there are specific signs when it's time to expand who is on board to get things done. Let's start from the perspective of an entrepreneur, boot-strapping it all to keep costs down.

You know it's time when your vision is to build a growing business and yet you find yourself living the following challenges:

- [ ] Your business is growing while your own business-building time is shrinking

- [ ] You have to turn away opportunities because you are so busy

- [ ] You are stuck at $X revenue and can't seem to get past that point

- [ ] You are still doing the same activities you were doing when you started your business.

- [ ] You have a great team, but find yourself frustrated by them always "bugging" you

Each of these signal that it's time to check your resistance, and check how you value your own time. After all YOU are the most valuable asset in your business. YOU are the Visionary and the one who will lead the team you'll put together.

Frankly, you shouldn't want to do it alone, because not only is it so much more fun to do it with support, but if you ever want to go on vacation and still grow your profits, you need a team.

"It is amazing what you can accomplish if you do not care who gets the credit."

~Harry S. Truman

More importantly, there are things that *you* shouldn't be spending time on in your business. However, the business needs those very things to be done. That is the point when you recognize *you just can't do it alone.*

These are the activities that drag you down and shut down your energy; they divert you from using your experience and expertise where it belongs - on 'growing' your business.

If you want to grow beyond 'just you in a private practice' (and especially if you want a multiple-6-Figure+ practice) you know you catch yourself doing distracting tasks - the tasks you use to keep you from working on the tough challenges you typically procrastinate doing. And the truth is: you're just not going to be able to grow without some support.

So first you must value yourself higher than you do right now.

CALCULATE YOUR VALUE FIRST

It sounds mundane, I know, but you need to step back and take pencil in hand... If your goal is to make $100,000 more next year, how many hours do you want to work to bring that in? Let's say you subtract the vacations and holidays and other obligations you want on your calendar. So you calculate it as 1,000 hours of your time ... thus $100 per hour of your time.

So if you're answering the phone, doing filing, talking to

clients about calendaring, that's work a $12 assistant could deliver while you spend your time on talking to clients about the next solution they need and finding joint venture partners.

And the same example holds if you're CEO of a million-dollars business, writing your marketing copy instead of having a $35 per hour marketing assistant do the first draft.

I encourage my clients to start "Breakthrough Small."

By that I mean, don't assume you 'must' hire full time employees. You can start by hiring exactly the perfect level of skill you need for the amount of work you want to hand off and pay for by your higher use of your own time.

For some, that means an Assistant for as little as $12 per hour for just five hours per week.

Even though it may not seem like a lot of time, there's so much that can be accomplished in five hours.

Just think about five hours full of things you don't want to do. Give them to someone else to complete, and imagine what would be possible for you to get done with those hours!

The same holds for valuing highly priced resources you need. My client **Nora** knew that she was about to start negotiating with a mega-corporation to provide her technology products to their customers. She needed sophisticated financial experience.

So the Breakthrough solution was buying 10 hours a week of a retired Chief Financial Officer who both helped set up her internal systems, and helped her strategize the business negotiations.

The great thing about hiring someone, even for just a few hours a week, is that you'll be sending the Universe a clear message that you do not want to run your business alone and that you're willing to accept help.

Now that you've gained back five hours of your life (and even recovered tons of energy because you're no longer drained by doing tasks you dislike), you can use that additional time and energy to shift your focus from administrative work to attracting more clients, and you'll see a huge return on your investment very quickly.

SUPPORT TEAMS

As you define your systems, you're defining the roles you need people to fulfill, the first steps of creating job descriptions. You'll find resources to guide that process in Appendixes A, B, and C. That system is exactly what you'll use now to look at the work you're going to hand off from the task level.

By going through all those steps, you have a description of the 'team' you're creating by the job descriptions you assemble.

Don't focus on the job titles yet - those can be changed if you need to as you meet potential hires and find out what they bring to the table - you'll build on what they can solve in addition to what you already know you want to delegate.

It's important to detail the expected job performance outcomes, and to be very specific in what is needed and expected. The job description should have 30-, 60-, 90- and 180-day objectives, so the candidate has a clear understanding of what is expected for the job. And so you know what you're evaluating!

Need an assistant? An implementer? A leader?

Do they need to be physically in your office? Or could they do their work for you remotely, by phone and Internet?

You need to know the specifics as the world of 'virtual assistants' has exploded in recent years - and widens your choices. Some of your tasks may be best handled by highly specialized resources that sell their work by the hour - consultants, vendors, experts-for-hire. They offer the highest expertise, for just the number of hours you need to solve things.

BREAKTHROUGH TEAM TIP 2

Keep looking until you find A+ people to hire.

Over and over I find clients trying to figure out the "1-Step System" for hiring fantastically skilled, experienced, capable high performers.

Remember the "red pill" that doesn't exist?

Well there is no "1-Step Hiring System" either.

Every single time someone complains to me about the mediocre or downright poor performance they're getting, not only are they avoiding managing that individual, but that person was also hired with a phantom 1-step process.

When I ask how they came to be hired I invariably hear "Judy knew them and said they're great and they seemed nice and smart when I talked to them for half an hour."

They hire the first nice smart person who walks in the door because it seems overwhelming to spend the energy to actually find a 'teammate' they can rely on to learn and perform well.

Is that really worth getting out of bed to go work with? I don't think so!

"What I do today is very important because I am exchanging a day of my life for it."

~ Paul "Bear" Bryant

It makes much more sense to build your team with stars instead – people who reduce your stress every day. My clients **Kevin and Ronny** both know – if it takes 2 months or 2 years to find the right manager to put in charge of a $10 million business unit, it's worth the time and the care. They'll be putting that person "in charge" of results.

One of the best ways to locate them is to… "Tell everyone you know" what the solution or service is that you're looking for. Sometimes it's called 'getting referrals.' As you obtain names from other people you can check the record of results and solutions they've produced for other people.

For some roles and responsibilities you may want to 'hire' commission-based headhunters who will do all the work of locating and screening candidates for you. OR shift a current employee into the 'new' position. For other roles you'll do it yourself. OK - I know, those are the words that have had you stalling and avoiding interviewing in the first place. Please stick with me here.

Most recently online resources have become a highly-used resource for posting positions - LinkedIn, Monster.com, Craig's List. It's a constantly shifting landscape of pathways to potential great hires.

However, I'll let you in on a secret. In 1990, 30% of open positions were filled by people who knew current employees of the company seeking to fill those positions.

In 2010 that figure had risen above 65%.

What that means is "Tell everyone you know!" because you never know who knows the person who could be your perfect solution. I tell my program members to use ALL available resources.

And that includes: "Tell everyone you know!"

Got it? Do it!

What's next?

Resumes, Resumes... Piles of Resumes

Soon in your hiring process, you will be faced with a big pile of resumes.

So how to make it through the piles? Look for resumes that already contain language and descriptions that match the specifics of your needs and notice the presentation style, which will tell you a great deal about the candidate.

It is helpful to decide what the priorities are for the position and look for those first in the resumes.

Once you have settled on a few resumes that seem like the 'best possible fit,' I suggest strongly that you use my two step approach to interviewing.

The first step is the telephone interview, which will save you valuable time and effort. Unfamiliar with interviewing? That's OK.

Ask the candidate a set of specific questions, such as:

- Why are you interested in this position?

- Please describe three key attributes that you have to offer to our company?

- Give me one significant program that you had an impact on in the last six months?

- Have you ever handled (a typical challenge you're tired of encountering in your own business)?

- How did you work on that? - What would you do differently if you had it to do again?

Listen carefully to the candidate to see if the response fits the job description, if their personality is one you like, if they seem to be a problem solver rather than a blamer. This process allows the candidate to earn a face-to-face interview.

Sort and rank the people you've spoken with and schedule face-to-face interviews with the best folks.

INTERVIEWING - THE ART OF LISTENING

When interviewing in person, it is important to listen and not let your emotions take over. Too often my clients find they've hired someone they 'liked' or 'resonated with'... Then, when that person isn't performing at the level they need to be, it can take months, years even to let them go so that the position can be filled by a better teammate.

The goal for interviewing effectively is to note your

candidate's thinking patterns, and not get caught up in appearances, impressive schools or companies. The best technique is one you've probably heard in many other settings: The candidate should talk about 80 percent of the interview and the interviewer only 20 percent.

During the interview, you'll want to use questions that are more specific and helpful in making successful hiring decisions.

Some directions to take your questions include:

- Ask what significant impact have they had (at three or more companies on their resumes)

- Ask for specifics, percentage of change and so on - concrete numbers whenever possible.

- Ask them to describe in detail what brought about the change

You're listening to learn what their process was, from A to Z, for solving problems and challenges that you have seen in the position, in your business, to see how they think, respond, take action.

Think about the experiences you've had over the years as a professional. What made *you* the most effective each time?

I venture to guess that one of the most helpful elements was having structure and definition to anchor your attention and efforts – understanding the purpose of everyone showing up and using all their time, intelligence and experience – knowing the goals and what 'success' would look like.

If you want each member of your team to be able to produce High Payoff results, you need to share your Vision and Goals with them. Then you need to spell out for them outline how their individual objects align to make those goals come true.

Don't keep it a secret. It becomes the starting point and the anchor for everyone's activity so repeat the Vision and Goals every chance you get.

So whether you are moving a current employee into a new role, or you are hiring a new staff member, your "kick-off" conversations should be identical!

BREAKTHROUGH TEAM TIP 3

Never use "mind-reading."

The reason I've spent so much time in this book outlining the Breakthrough path from Vision through Action is because it's based on a pattern that you can repeat over and over again.

Set your Vision for being a confident leader and manager.

Convert it into Goals.

Share the Vision and Goals with others so they can bring their best efforts to accomplishing them.

Any time I hear someone say "It's obvious" or "Everyone knows…" or "I don't have time to show someone else how to do it" I know it's time for a figurative kick in the pants.

It's NEVER obvious until people have worked together for thousands of hours with hundreds of projects and problem solving conversations where their ideas and ways of thinking have already been shared.

So MAKE THE TIME – in regular business meetings and each Delegation Meeting you'll hold with people on their first day, and the schedule of check ins you'll use as well.

All of these examples have been from the types of teams you'll construct to get work done. There's another type of team that I believe is as critical to your success.

ADVISORY TEAMS

What challenges would you like to leap over?

I mean, if there were three paths to success they'd likely be called "Learn it the hard way", "Learn it the easy way" and "Get handed the answer on a silver platter."

Everyone should have his 'silver platter' team as well.

BREAKTHROUGH PRINCIPLE 4

CHALLENGES MELT AWAY...
WHEN YOU SURROUND YOURSELF WITH TEAMS,
MODELS AND MENTORS

The best athletes and business leaders have one thing in common: great coaches. Friends and family often tell us what they think we want to hear... or what will keep us from getting too 'different' from them and their results.

That's not the path to Breakthroughs.

One of the core reasons to work with consultants, coaches, mentors and mastermind programs is to gain access to tens of thousands of hours of experience and expertise embodied in other people.

When you join these programs you know you're joining like-minded business people – those who want to bring their gifts and intelligence to creating conditions for Breakthroughs for each other.

Nothing busts our assumptions as fast as another point of view. And the best place to get them busted is when you get together with other people you trust to be your supporters.

Find yourself mastermind programs and mentors - these are the folks who have your best interests in mind as they give you their experience and input to shortcut your path.

If you'd like information about the masterminds I run for entrepreneurs and business owners, go to **www.feinholz.com** or call **1-877-929-5989** for details.

I encourage you to make the Breakthrough decision to surround yourself with people who can reflect back to you the limiting beliefs and assumptions you may be using, as well as handing you unbiased ideas and opinions, all for the purpose of helping YOU succeed.

CASE STUDIES

My client **Nora** grew her business by staging her hiring of fulltime employees - first a technical support person to answer client questions so she could continue to focus on product design and creation. Next, a programmer who could do half the new product development.

With time freed up, she doubled her sales, and again added tech support and programmers. Then she added marketing staff.

Her Breakthrough Result: she grew from a solo-programmer to a multi-million-dollar business with a team of 27.

Shannon grew her business by partnering up with semi-retired peers, experienced experts in her industry. She focused on selling their combined offerings while they staffed the on-site work, and she used interns to handle the marketing and administration tasks.

The result: doubling the business in four years.

Darren managed a hundred-million-dollar manufacturing operation. He had no time to spend on sorting out the strategy for the company - key issues languished for two years.

By defining what the highest and best use of HIS experience and time was, we built the business case to bring on two new management staff, one by promoting from within.

Darren's Breakthrough Result: within three months, he was on planes to Europe and Asia, dealing with strategic partnering issues, and coaching his new plant manager by phone, and in person when he was back at the headquarters.

Nick began with the assumption he had to grow his business.

Nick's Breakthrough results: He brought his son into the business to begin learning the industry, the products and customers. With a 10-year plan to turn the business over to his son, Nick could focus on fine-tuning the current business to add profits to his savings, enjoy his business and love his life.

Tamara moved to France and used the home study course and our bonus phone strategy sessions to launch her $25,000 per person coaching program.

Different Breakthroughs, matching the different Visions and Goals each of them had for themselves.

BACK TO YOU

Make a point of making a list of everything you wish you could hand off to another person, and prioritize the list. Select the least risky or most urgent to fill – it's your choice!

My Ah Ha's

☐

☐

☐

☐

☐

Don't let Team Building be your "rock of Sisyphus." Take action on your Breakthrough Team Building Block's Action Plan.

BREAKTHROUGH ACTION PLAN

☐ Identify 3 projects you're not getting to

☐ List each of the ways they would add value to your business and accomplish your Vision and Goals

☐ Develop a job description for the role that could accomplish what needs doing

☐ List who you'll notify of the opening

☐ Coordinate with a business attorney or human resources advisor exactly how to make the offer to your selected candidate

☐ Review the Delegation Meeting system to draft how you'll conduct that discussion with the person you are going to task with the new job assignment

☐ Design how you'll train others to use the new system and monitor the results you're getting

See www.BreakthroughByDesign.com/gold

EIGHT
EIGHT
EIGHT

SUPPORT

Every Breakthrough can be traced back to its Source after the fact. But how do we start from where we are now and move forward, deliberately creating Breakthroughs?

In nearly 30 years of helping people struggling with overwhelm get 'unstuck' and leaping into the successes they want to create, I've uncovered several specific conditions that enable Breakthroughs to show up *and* be perceived.

You can think of these as creating reliable structures that frame and hold all the other Building Blocks by devoting attention to both your Inner Wiring (skills) and your Outer Environment (support) – Building Blocks of their own.

"We must overcome the notion that we must be regular – it robs you of the chance to be extraordinary and leads you to the mediocre."

~ Uta Hagen

Let's start with the inside, shall we? The foundation of all Breakthroughs is your openness to experience them.

We start as infants exploring the world, but most of us become trained to try to fit in. That means our habit is to try to stick with the 'familiar', with what we tell ourselves that we 'know'. Even when we say we want different results, all too often we revert to taking the same actions, or only look at options that fit the way we already experience the world.

Sometimes out of fear, usually just plain habit, we create blindness to options we could use to get different results.

So what to do?

EXPAND YOUR POINTS OF VIEW

Do you want to rely on the happenstance of a lucky mind shift, or create a flexible mindset? Since there's no telling when the first will take place, I vote for the second.

It's like saying I love sports and I want to know how to do more than flag football and folk dancing.

You need to get yourself out of your habits and repetitive ways of experiencing the world by exposing yourself to ideas and frameworks you're not used to using.

> **"Mental flexibility unbends the bent, unties the knot, and unsticks the stuck."**
>
> **~ Liz Strauss**

My own explorations have taken me through years of reading hundreds of books, and investing in training courses - programs like Byron Katie's work, the Star's Edge courses, materials from many other consciousness training programs.

And reading - lots of material that has nothing to do with what I 'already know'. Mind expanding rather than affirming.

The result: I see hundreds of possibilities when I'm working with my clients and can offer them a host of different approaches and ideas to learn and make their own.

Make it your habit to subscribe to magazines that have nothing to do with your business or industry. Take yourself to a retreat center or belief busting experience. Shift yourself!

OWN YOUR TIME

The first personal quality necessary to achieve Breakthrough success is that you must master and take control of your time.

Time is an expendable commodity. Each one of us has the same 24 hours in each day. When those hours are gone, they cannot be replaced. They are gone forever, never recaptured.

You must treat your time as precious, and guard it wisely and selfishly. Don't let anyone disrupt you or take you away from the focus you have on your goals.

But it's more than "time" we're talking about. It's Attention. If you let others draw you away from your goals, you are simply saying that their goals are more important than your own and it's more valuable to use your attention on their goals than yours.

BREAKTHROUGH PRODUCTIVITY TIP 1

"People who don't have goals are used by people who do."

If you are serious about business success – really serious, then this is one of the most important and critical areas to defend. One key way to regain control over your attention is a technique I teach my coaching program members to use – Time Blocking.

On your calendar, create a single topic appointment with yourself and give it a topic, and the result you're working towards. Turn off your email, ignore inbound phone calls and don't let people interrupt with a "quick question."

For **Darren** that meant 2-hour working blocks. For **Leonard**, that meant 45-minute blocks with 15-minute periods for answering emails and voice mails and incoming calls.

It always sounds like an odd idea, and yet I get calls from clients saying "I didn't want to do it but committed to try it. I had a project I was sure would take 2 hours – and at the 40 minute mark I realized I'd completed it and started work on another project and made even more headway!"

Use Time Blocking once a day or twenty times a week.

If you want to create Breakthroughs for entire teams, I challenge you to cut your meetings down to 27 minutes.

Why? Because it's weird and it keeps people on their toes and focused on the topic that needs discussion.

BUILD YOUR SKILLS

Back when I was consulting to Walt Disney Imagineering I noticed that what made the team such fun to be with was their continual investment in learning. They were committed to getting their "rock of Sisyphus" out of the way each time they spotted it.

Artists kept taking art classes. Architects and engineers worked on projects that demanded new solutions. The computer support staff was constantly asked for new ways of solving matters.

Every discipline was continuously being challenged and coming up with new solutions. So each and every one of them was constantly learning. No matter your professional discipline, if you want Breakthroughs you need to keep learning, expanding how you problem-solve, how you interact with your team.

Enroll yourself in training programs that have a curriculum and assignments so that each thing you learn gets put in practice immediately - that's how new skills become your own new habits. Invest in yourself and your success.

Work with coaches and consultants and join mastermind groups specifically so that you can get regular exposure to many points of view.

ACKNOWLEGE BREAKTHROUGHS EVERY TIME

As I was finalizing the final draft of this book I received a phone call from my client **DeeDee**. It was the morning after a 3-hour conversation about her next steps in increasing her disciplined use of time and attention balancing her work commitments, her spiritual practices, and her travel for pleasure.

"I just have to tell you that the framework you shared last night was worth the entire retainer. With that one sentence I completely let go of that old attachment. Wow. I'm seeing it all completely differently along with all my new choices."

I haven't told her, but after we hung up from our call, I did a happy dance around the office!

BREAKTHROUGH PRINCIPLE 5

YOU'LL BREAK THROUGH AGAIN...
WHEN YOU SYSTEMIZE TAKING ACTION ON THEM AND
CELEBRATE THE ONE YOU JUST MADE

Decide ahead of time how you'll reward yourself each time you have a Breakthrough – there's nothing like one celebration to encourage another.

Nick took his family on weekend camping trips as a reward to himself for each of his Breakthrough.

Jack bought himself the next tech toy he had his eye on after each Breakthrough as a way to keep himself committed to creating the circumstances and focus on having them.

Karen used photography retreats to both trigger her Breakthroughs and celebrate each one.

For some people, their celebration looks a lot like a reward.

For others their celebrations are focused on sharing their new insights and "Ah Ha!"s with their teams, and turning those into celebratory events. In that way, they use the 'launch' of the new insight as a celebration just as much as the achievement of the new Vision or Goals that are designed and accomplished.

One of my mastermind members schedules a spa day for her entire team (women all).

Another rented out an entire movie screening for his team of a hot Summer film release.

It's all up to your and your team's imagination as to what a 'celebration' could be.

I'm such a seminar junkie that I use the desire to go to another one as my incentive to set aside the time to focus on something that has me stuck, before I go to the conference. Then I get the double joy of having the event both as my celebration, and as the booster shot for even more new insights.

Neat trick, isn't it? I know you can see the interaction between these two Building Blocks of Inner Wiring and Outer Environment in each of these examples, as well as the sections above.

So your next assignment is to define the Foundation elements of skills building and support that you want to put in place and the steps you'll use to move from there through the rest of the topics discussed above.

Create the conditions that will enable you to invite Breakthroughs in, and the steps you'll use to keep your attention on sustaining those conditions.

Among your tools are using appointments with yourself on the calendar, booking yourself into mastermind meetings at set intervals, taking courses so that you have to meet regular assignment deadlines, and so on.

CASE STUDIES

Susan, Nick, Karen, Jennifer, Elaine, Paul, Darren, Nora, Tamara, Jack, Jacob, Elliot, Leonard, Roseanne, Shannon, all made the decision to get support. They did it in different forms and often using more than one source of support:

- ☐ Private consulting services to handle multiple issues

- ☐ Mastermind groups with weekly meeting agendas and round robin discussions of each participant's

- ☐ Online self guided programs

- ☐ Coaching individually and with their teams

- ☐ Advisory Boards and Mentors

Their objective was simple: create a business they love and a life they adore, more money, more fun. Their "New Normal."

BACK TO YOU

As you think about the support you want from a Mentor or Board of Advisors, don't forget to list the people you'll want to include in the design of solutions and the celebrations of your successes.

There's nothing like sharing the good news to keep you heading back for the next... Breakthrough!

If you know you're ready to get support from those who have been there before you, get yourself into a Breakthrough program like the ones described above: individual coaching, working with a consultant on your business, using home study courses, etc.

My Ah Ha's

☐

☐

☐

☐

☐

☐

☐

Here's your final Action Plan, for creating the Foundation of your Skills and Support on an ongoing basis.

BREAKTHROUGH ACTION PLAN

- ☐ Identify at least 2 sources you'll use to set conditions for creating Breakthroughs and making them your "New Normal"

- ☐ List 2 ways you'll expand your mindset

- ☐ Locate 3 ways you'll build your skills

- ☐ Calendar the time blocking you'll use to focus without interruptions each day

- ☐ Decide on the resources you'll use as your advisors and how often you'll meet with them

- ☐ Calendar when you'll contact them to update them and get their input

- ☐ Decide how and when you'll celebrate your Breakthroughs in business and in life

See www.BreakthroughByDesign.com/gold

The topics covered above are covered in more depth, with CDs, online audio and videos, action guides and coaching programs in Your Business Breakthrough System.

Learn more about the Breakthrough online courses and programs at www.BreakthroughByDesign.com/gold

NINE
NINE
NINE

BREAKTHROUGH
ACTION

I wish I could have you in my life for two years. Why? Because in that time I know we'd transform you from Vision through Action, you'd master all the Breakthrough tools and building blocks I share here and make them your "New Normal."

As I pulled my thoughts together for this final chapter I realized that one of the best gifts I can share with you is to reveal one of the private methods I use for inviting Breakthroughs. I have a secret trick I haven't discussed with anyone before this.

Even my best friends in business and in life didn't know it.

Those of us who want Breakthroughs face the challenge of how our consciousness works, balancing 'being on automatic' with 'being aware' for limited spans of time. We have to outsmart our default: unconsciousness. Consciousness tries to push through as we stubbornly resist one thought or action, insist on another, having running 'un'-consciousness conversations.

I've learned to use 'wake up' shouts at my Conscious Awareness because I *know* I keep 'forgetting' the...

The 4 C's of BREAKTHROUGHS

COURAGE

+

CURIOSITY

+

CONDITIONS

+

COMMITMENT

=

BREAKTHROUGH

When I lose sight of these 4 C's, these 4 States, I end up wandering in circles "thinking about" things rather than looking at what has me stuck, making decisions and taking action.

So I use tricks to trigger awakenings, to point out I'm stalled on something, so that I consciously Breakthrough to solve it.

I call these tricks my awareness "Sneakthrough" tools. I set them up to operate 'on automatic' like partners, set up on purpose. Having them makes waking myself up inevitable.

Here's one example of how I set up Sneakthroughs.

For 27 months I happened to have one film on my digital video recording system. When it got erased I realized I'd been using it for three different purposes.

Each time I scrolled through the recordings list (nearly daily) the title winks at me and reminds me of the Breakthrough trigger ideas it contains. Every once in a while, I watched the entire movie just for the sheer fun and pleasure of all the energy it contains. Then, I left the recording rolled forward and paused on a specific scene in the movie where the conversation is all about Breakthroughs in perception, Visioning, personal Goal setting, making choices and taking action.

That movie is *Matrix*, and the scene is the one in which Morpheus holds out his hand to Neo and offers him the 'red pill' – the one that triggers waking up out of his illusions into Life.

Instant wisdom, instant insight, instant Breakthroughs all in one pill.

And that pill doesn't exist. What does exist is a host of tools, techniques, mechanisms, systems, and devices to wake our Selves up and remind us of our Vision and commitments to ourselves.

The Matrix reminder is one device that works for me. Instant reminder to me to 'wake up', just knowing that was the scene on 'pause.' So I searched for the film and rerecorded it. It's sitting there as I write this.

Another Sneakthrough tool is the front screen on my cell phone – I don't need to see a kids face or lily in my koi pond – I do need help staying focused on my priorities, so I customized it to flash reminders to me each time I turn it on.

BE A BREAKTHROUGH MASTER

Knowing how easy it is for me to be distracted by interruptions, questions, mind blips, there are probably ten different quick tools, deliberate ones as well as Sneakthrough tools, I use during my week to remind me of the actions I've said I'm going to take.

All my techniques are in service of one key challenge:

"HOW will I keep myself in Action, committed to Breakthrough follow through and make it my New Normal?"

So what tools, Sneakthrough or otherwise will YOU use?

Why am I so committed to this? Let me share with you what motivates me. My core value in life is unleashing potential so it makes its positive difference for others and the world.

So to accomplish *my* Vision and Goals, I need *you* to accomplish yours. Your Vision, your Actions have a domino effect in the world. You become the mentor and model others are waiting for. Each of your Breakthroughs shows other people that they can create theirs too! As you model curiosity, Breakthroughs and actions, you show others they can transform their business, their life and the world.

Here's a "booster" Principle I've uncovered: The more companions we surround ourselves with, share our journey with, who share our desire to bring our best into the world, the easier it becomes.

BREAKTHROUGH "BOOSTER" PRINCIPLE

BREAKTHROUGH MASTERS ...
WANT COMPANIONS FOR THE JOURNEY

I told you how **Susan's** path went from stuck for years, to making her first Breakthrough in 17 days, and her third in 3 days. She began to believe she could indeed create a very different path to the results she wanted. And she made it true!

It doesn't require elaborate ceremonies or complex retreats. It just requires using the Building Block sequence – See a Vision, Set a Goal, Identify the obstacles, steps and resources and new practices, design them, declare them, do them. DONE!

Even a Mentor has mentors.

Ten years ago, I had issues that I chewed on for months or years. It might have taken days or weeks to look at them and to solve them. My 'fed up' lead me to look for answers: I studied and searched and tried on 1,000s of techniques, got myself mentors who helped me triangulate in on which methods worked best for my style, and so on. I kept at it until I had a set that work for me, for my students and clients and readers.

It didn't stop at that point.

I'm committed to never staying stuck ever again. So I work with 2 or more mentors every year, investing tens of thousands of dollars.

And each time I commit to that work, my business and my life take leaps forward. That's how I've created a profit model for my own business that doubled in a year, and is on track to doubling again.

It's as a result of working with mentors that I've been able to do for myself what I want to do for you: take Vision and Goals and passions and expertise and turn them into a lucrative stream of income and turn the profits from that model into a life I adore and use to make a difference in my community and the world.

Some of my mentors are also my mentees. We know the investment we make pays off richly in the speed of Breakthroughs that are available to us.

BREAKTHROUGH PRINCIPLE 4

CHALLENGES MELT AWAY...
WHEN YOU SURROUND YOURSELF WITH TEAMS,
MODELS AND MENTORS

Now, when I become aware of overwhelm and stall outs,

when I realize I'm stuck, I can make one phone call to a Breakthrough Buddy and talk it all through out loud in about 3 minutes flat. And I do the same thing for them. It's another version of Team that we create for ourselves, and you remember what I shared before:

You picked up this book because you were fed up feeling stuck. It's time you got yourself both the Building Blocks AND Breakthrough Buddies, companions for your journey.

One way is to get yourself into a Breakthrough program like the ones described above: masterminds, individual coaching, working with a consultant on your business, using home study courses, etc.

Who have your mentors been? Which support are you ready to *get* now? This book is one way I can mentor you. My on-line study courses, masterminds, coaching and consulting are others. It's my passion to mentor action takers who want support achieving their Vision. How will you take action to get support and create your Breakthroughs? Decide NOW, and take action NOW!

BE A BREAKTHROUGH MENTOR

Which support are you ready to *give* to others?

One small step I'd like you to take is to expand your Vision of who you are, and BE the mentor to others. Introduce them to the ideas in this book, create time blocks for discussing what you may be pondering or stalled on, and use the tools in these chapters with each other.

If you've found value in this book, if you've learned something that's making a difference for you, consider giving five copies to people you care about, whom you wish to help on their path to Breakthrough success in business and in Life.

They might be colleagues, friends, family members, vendors, team members, golf buddies, or someone you meet on vacation – anyone curious to learn and grow, anyone you see is stalled out.

Write down five people you will give a copy of this book to:

1. _____

2. _____

3. _____

4. _____

5. _____

Your helping someone else create Breakthroughs in their business and life is a key step to *your* owning the insights you've gained and your commitment to using these tools.

BE YOUR OWN CASE STUDY

So here's the scoop. Amazing opportunities surround you. You get access to them by making each new tool a regular part of your life, and by being a Breakthrough Master!

Your success inspires me to continue my work and it inspires others too! I want to know the difference you want to make in the world and how it's coming along for you.

How have the ideas in this book, your Ah Ha's, your Breakthroughs, and Action Plans helped you?

What Visions have you unveiled? What Goals have you set?

Here's your final Action Plan, for creating the Foundation of your Skills and Support on an ongoing basis.

BREAKTHROUGH ACTION PLAN

- ☐ Identify at least 2 "Sneakthrough" tools you'll use to remind you about Breakthroughs
- ☐ Gift 5 people with Breakthrough books
- ☐ Send Linda success stories
- ☐ Decide on the Breakthrough Buddies you want to include
- ☐ Decide who you want to Mentor and do it!

What new Actions did you take? What Results have you created?

Send Me Your Success Stories

- ☐ If you've been overwhelmed, what Breakthrough shifted it for you? If you've been stalled, what Ah Ha's got you moving again?
- ☐ What Vision did you shape for yourself? What Goals did you set and Actions have you used to make progress toward it?
- ☐ What results have you created and how have you celebrated your Breakthroughs?

Send it to www.success@TheBreakthroughBook.com

Susan, Nick, Karen, Jennifer, Elaine, Paul, Darren, Nora, Tamara, Jack, Jacob, Leonard, Roseanne, Shannon, Kevin and Ronny - all of them offered their stories to you.

They all appreciate how much they learned from and were inspired by the stories other entrepreneur and business owners, my other clients and students, shared with them.

Each insight, each action, each result *you* create is powerful.

I want *your* success stories and testimonials because they help me help others. This book could change the course of another person's life – that's the gift you can be for them.

Remember the mentors who have gifted you along the way? Do not hesitate to Be A Mentor and a catalyst in the life of others on your journey.

Thank you for investing your valuable time in learning new ways to boost the results you are creating in the world, and giving yourself access to the infinite opportunities that await you. I love knowing that I have companions on my journey who share my Vision of taking your passion, your gifts, your experience and expertise and using it to make a life you adore and a difference in the world.

I look forward to reading your success story.

Here's to YOUR Breakthrough Success!

Linda Feinholz

When you become a Leader, success is all about growing others." ~Jack Welch

**MOTIVATE AND INSPIRE OTHERS
TO CREATE THEIR BREAKTHROUGHS
"SHARE THIS BOOK"**

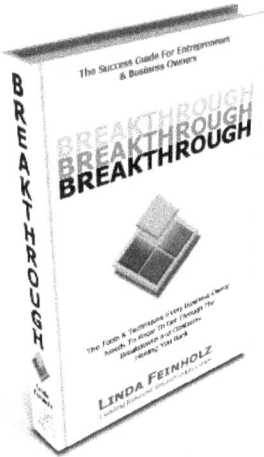

BREAKTHROUGH:

**The Success Guide for
Entrepreneurs & Business Owners**

The Tools & Techniques Every
Business Owner Needs To Know
To Get Through The Breakdowns
and Obstacles Holding You Back

*Includes: Breakthrough Action Plan
Guides and live program certificate*

List Price: $27.95

Special Quantity Discounts

3 - 20 Books	$24.95 each
21 - 99 Books	$21.95 each
100 - 499 Books	$18.95 each
500 - 999 Books	$15.95 each
1,000+ Books	$13.95 each

**To place an order call 1-877-929-5989
or visit www.TheBreakthroughBook.com**

Appendix A
KNOW THE VALUE OF
PLEASING YOUR CUSTOMERS

As a business owner, you must thrill your customers, and build trust in you and your business.

So each and every activity in your business is WORTH the investment of your time and your team to figure out how to deliver enormous satisfaction with the least effort for the long run - so it becomes your choice who you have as clients.

The effort of systematizing feels like a distraction and an expense, and unfortunately, most business owners simply don't understand it.

Let's take a look at what the potential cost could be to you if you fail to do these things:

Let's say that you make $200 in sales per year from your average customer.

And let's say that for any number of reasons, 100 customers stop doing business with you each year. They may die or move away. They may no longer have need for your products or services, they may switch companies, have a relative in the business, or possibly have a bad experience with someone in your company.

Or, they may just simply disagree with some policy or procedure you might have.

It could be a falling out with a staff member or employee, personality conflict, miscommunication, a problem they had with one of your products, or perhaps a feeling of neglect from you or someone in your business.

You notice I'm not talking about your product or service - it's about everything else they may encounter!

It really doesn't matter what the reason, they just stop doing business with you.

Well, those 100 customers no longer paying you $200 this year just cost you $20,000.

But, that's not all. What if those 100 customers tell 5 others about their experience with you?

You think telling "5" is an exaggeration?

Here's a lesson learned by one of the world's premier marketers: The Disney Company.

Statistically, for every individual guest in one of their theme parks on a given day who is so annoyed by something they experienced that they walk all the way back to the Main Gate, to fill out and turn in a complaint card…

400 other people feel the exact same way that very day.

That's 399 who don't bother to use their time communicating their dissatisfaction.

These are the people who don't divert their time and energy to let you know when they're not pleased - they just take their future business elsewhere.

So for you that means that's an additional 500 potential customers who won't be doing business with you this year (or maybe ever, for that matter).

And if each of them spent an average of $200, that's $100,000 you won't be receiving from them, *PLUS* the $20,000 you lost on your existing customers who left.

That brings the total in lost income to *$120,000 in just one year!*

It's not unusual for some businesses to bring in a hundred (or more) new customers each month.

That's twelve hundred-plus, customers a year. And they end up only netting a 150 or 200 increase at year-end (sometimes not even that).

Well, what happened to the other more than 1,000 customers? Where did they go? Surely, they all didn't die, or move away.

So first there was the original marketing effort and expense, and then the cost of getting acquainted with that customer, and now you get to spend those dollars all over again!

But, you know, most business owners don't concern themselves with what, or whom they've lost.

They just focus on their net gain.

They figure that if they finish the year with more customers or more sales than they started with, they're ahead.

Now, let's suppose that you gave those 100 lost customers reasons - good, compelling, life or business enhancing reasons, to continue doing business with you this year.

And let's suppose each of them told those same five people about their now-positive experience with you.

Well, there's $20,000 you wouldn't have lost in the first place, and another $100,000 you may possibly pick up from their referrals or by their word of mouth.

KNOW YOUR NUMBERS

The point is, customers are important – *all* customers. In fact, they're critical. There's no question about it.

You and I both know that.

A business couldn't remain in business unless it has someone to buy its products and services.

Those "someones" are people. Real people. People like you and like me. If you sell your products to the business community, remember, businesses don't buy from businesses.

People in business buy from other people in business. It's people that you market to. Not businesses.

EVERYONE TALKS

You think your customers aren't talking to your prospects? In this day of Internet message boards, forums, comments and so on, let alone the millions of visitors to trade shows and conventions it's even MORE likely that comments about your company and team are making the rounds.

In one month alone I stood in the aisle of a conference trade show and plainly overheard comments about a company whose representatives were 40 feet away.

I then overheard comments made by people standing in line at a weekend vegetable market, commenting on the vendors who had booths there, and commenting about retailers across the street.

Appendix B
DESIGNING SYSTEMS

What is it that you can do, *specifically*, to extend your customer's buying lifetime with you?

What system for not only marketing and delivering service but retaining customers need to be put in place?

And as you start this process ask yourself who else should you bring in to participate in it?

Take yourselves through the following questions:

1. **Which Activities Will We Do More Than Once?**

2. **How Many Steps Does It Take To Get Each One Done Well?**

3. **How Many Steps Could Be Removed To Make It Easier To Do While Improving The Result?**

4. **How Many People Touch This Process?**

5. **How Could We Do It Even More Effectively With Fewer People Or Fewer Touches?**

6. **What Parts Of This Could Be Automated?**

7. **What Parts Of This Could Be Delegated?**

8. **What Aspects Of This Could Be Out-sourced?**

Track how many times activities are done, and how long each step takes. Develop a work plan to take the best ideas for doing it 'better' deeper and more detailed.

Appendix C
TURNING SYSTEMS INTO
JOB DESCRIPTIONS

Here's the secret to creating systems AND job descriptions for your business:

Gather your team together and ask these questions:

1. What is your job - your primary function? How would you describe your position to a new hire?

2. What do you do all day?

3. What are you responsible for?

4. Who are you accountable to? Who is accountable to you?

5. Approximately how much time do you spend on of your tasks?

6. Where are you being most effective? Least effective?

7. What is working well? Not well? Could be working better?

Repeat this for each person in the company.

Import their answers into two systems:

A - Their job descriptions, and

B - The list of activities in the business.

Now, to create the job descriptions, document the following:

Who does what? Who's responsible and/or accountable for what?

What is the location where the work takes place? (At home? At the office?

Are any special tools (computer? fax machine?) required? Who supplies them?

What is the required physical space like? What education and previous experience is required to do each job?)

Next, What are the physical and social requirements (e.g., lifting? language? driving?) What special skills, certifications or abilities are needed? (proficiencies with specific computer programs? great phone voice? math skills? languages?)

The next step is for each person - including the boss - to keep a *Daily Tracking Log* for one week.

For five days each of you will write down the specific tasks that you do - just notes; this isn't a diary.

You'll be able to see if jobs are being duplicated and how much time is being spent on each.

Create a simple form that will work for every position.

This can be a form that allows for 15-30 minute time blocks and short notations.

Now it's time to actually create written job descriptions for everyone in the company.

Oops, are you a one-man-band or a one-woman-show? No problem.

If that's the case, you will write up job descriptions for each of the jobs that either *should* exist or will... someday.

Plan for growth.

Yes, you may be doing everything right now, but when the time comes - as you grow - you will be replacing yourself.

So prepare for it now by writing up those job descriptions so that you will know what you are looking for down the road.

It's much easier to fill a position when you know what you are looking for...

And for the second step - Document your Systems

From those notes you've been taking you can now write the steps used to accomplish each activity to refine your task level descriptions as Training Materials for new hires or people to whom you are about to assign the work.

You can also use those notes to design the job descriptions to post ads, and to use during interviewing, and to convert into performance evaluation forms, and so on.

Appendix D
5 Meetings Defined

Ad Hoc - Also known as a 'Hallway Meeting' or "Open Door Interruption' – unplanned and unprepared for. Usually initiated by the phrase "This will only take a second..." While it often expedites decision-making for one person, the interruption generally disrupts the concentration and workflow of the other person.

Delegation / Performance Management - Planned and prepared for. A sequence of discussions to clarify and reach agreement about the goal of the assignment, the support that will be sought and given as the new responsibilities are assumed, the schedule of status meetings about the progress being made, and the review and evaluation that will take place in a scheduled manner.

Status - A scheduled meeting with 3 agenda points: transmission of information regarding ongoing initiatives and issues; information needed that can only be provided by the individuals in the meeting, and notice of an issue or paradox needing a Working Session.

Working Session - A single-topic scheduled meeting. Each participant is notified of the information they are to prepare and bring for the meeting. All issues raised during the meeting that are off-topic are captured on a Parking Lot list for resolution at the meeting's conclusion or at a separate time.

Presentation / Training - Generally used for passing information and providing a public forum for posing questions and additional ideas to advance the matter at hand. Needs a tight agenda to prevent people's distraction with other matters and technology interruptions. It may also be paired with a Brainstorming session, identifying issues for future discussion.

Appendix E
How To Hold Effective Meetings

There are several questions you need to answer in order to set up and run an effective meeting.

Which topics should be routinely discussed versus on an as needed basis? How long should meetings take – 5 minutes, 15 minutes? What about ad hoc meetings? Are the right people being invited to each meeting? How often have you been to meetings and wondered why you are there? Are meetings too often, too long and often useless?

To answer these questions, follow the steps for designing meetings that work.

1. **Have an agenda** that notes the objectives and how you will meet them in the meeting. Send it out before the meeting to everyone involved so they can prepare.

2. **Set a start AND ending time** – and stick to both. If you get into the habit of starting meetings on time those perennial latecomers will force themselves to show up on time. Ending on time earns you the respect of everyone. They know they can count on you to get them out on time.

3. Have only the **people** in the meeting that really need to be there. This should be either because their area impacts or is impacted by the topic under discussion, or because they have some expertise or knowledge that is needed for the discussion.

4.   **Notify** the participants of materials you want them to bring so they can come **prepared** to participate fully.

5.   Have someone be accountable for the **time** and getting through the agenda. If you want to participate fully in the discussions, use someone else as the **facilitator**.

6.   Do not let anyone pull you off the agenda and sidetrack the meeting. **Stay on track.** Make notes of other topics raised on a "Parking Lot". Review them at the end of the meeting, assign them, and schedule other meetings to handle them.

7.   A 5-minute, stand-up **briefing daily** with your direct reports can cut hours of time that would otherwise be lost with one-on-ones that you would have to have, or lost time by your staff because of waiting perhaps all day or longer to get a question answered.

8.   If you think a meeting is going to take more than 27 minutes, take another look at your objectives. If you **limit the meeting** to 27 minutes, you set the tone for people to be brief and to the point, come prepared and pay attention. You are also more likely to get everyone there that you want. Longer meetings should be the exception rather than the rule.

A constant flow of information going in all directions – up, down, and across is essential. Do not leave it to chance.

Plan it.

Manage it.

Enjoy it!

Appendix F
7 Steps To Solve Any Issue

Step 1 - AGREE what the issue is that needs to be solved.

83% of the time, I find my clients are already implementing something that is solving the wrong issue, and no one will stop because they can't figure out how to express what their gut is telling them. "This isn't the actual thing we need fixed."

Step 2 - AGREE what the criteria will be for determining when it's solved

Sounds redundant, I know.

But most of the time, half of the input was missing from the beginning so the solution is half-baked, and will satisfy only one or two people while everyone else says "What's the point of raising the issue, no one is listening."

So hundreds of hours and thousands of dollars get spent and the 'solution' is useless and unused.

Step 3 - DECIDE what needs to be researched before any recommendations are made

Yes, research. Who has tried solving this issue before? What are some best practices for doing this that exist? What's out there before we start trying to design it from scratch?

Step 4 - REVIEW the options you uncover as solutions with the stakeholders in case you find out that #1 or #2 needs to be modified...

If SO, take it from the top, so that the recommendations you'll be evaluating are the best possible choices.

... only then **Evaluate and Select your preferred solution**.

Step 5 - Assign your design team to put the PLAN together.

Yes, the plan.

Don't grumble at me.

The reason that the information technology world produces projects that work is because of the 80-20 Rule - spend 80 percent of your effort up front and 20 percent in implementation and it will work!

Get organized before you get in Action.

Step 6 - Implement the Plan

I'll leave it to you to fill in these steps - it's not a project planning systems book, after all!

Step 7 - Test and Adjust!

I'll forever be grateful for the time I spent working with the management teams of Walt Disney Imagineering.

The reason Disney theme parks deliver stellar entertainment experiences with consummate safety is because they never assume what they have implemented is final - they are always tracking and checking in to see if the experience is what was intended from the start...

And everyone pitches in to give useful constructive feedback so it can be improved on continuously.

www.ingramcontent.com/pod-product-compliance
Lightning Source LLC
Chambersburg PA
CBHW060024210326

41520CB00009B/990